STRENGTH FOR TODAY, HOPE FOR TOMORROW

LIVING HOPE CHRISTIAN CENTER

Printed in the United States of America

Table Of Contents

DEDICATION

We would like to dedicate this book to the people of
Jefferson County whom we love and serve.

ACKNOWLEDGEMENTS

I would like to thank the people of Living Hope Christian Center for their boldness and vulnerability in telling the stories that comprise this compilation of real-life stories.

This book would not have been published without the amazing efforts of our project manager, Diane Popenhagen. Her untiring resolve pushed this project forward and turned it into a stunning victory. Thank you for your great fortitude and diligence. I would also like to thank our invaluable proofreader, Melody Davis, for all the focus and energy she has put into perfecting our words. Lastly, I want to extend our gratitude to Evan Earwicker, our graphic artist, whose talent and vision continually astound us. We are so blessed to have you as a part of this team.

Daren Lindley
President and CEO
Good Catch Publishing

The book you are about to read
is a compilation of authentic life stories.
The facts are true, and the events are real.
These storytellers have dealt with crisis, tragedy, abuse
and neglect and have shared their most private moments,
mess-ups and hang-ups in order for others to learn and
grow from them. In order to protect the identities of those
involved in their pasts, the names and details of some
storytellers have been withheld or changed.

INTRODUCTION

A Spring in the Desert
By Melanie Widmer

Everyone has a story. Some people are full of them: tall tales, fish stories, embarrassing moments, tales of love and loss. Every once in a while, there's a story that wedges itself into our hearts and helps us see things from a new perspective.

This book contains seven stories, true stories, about people who live right here in Jefferson County. You might even know them. Maybe you've chatted with them in the checkout line; maybe your kids are on the same little league team. These people's lives have been shaken by abuse, drugs, homelessness, mental illness and more. But you'll find one thing in common through all the stories: hope. There *is* a peace that passes understanding.

Even when we're under the crushing weight of despair, when all seems lost, there is hope.

I will never leave you or forsake you.
~God
(Deuteronomy 31:6)

A PLACE TO CALL HOME
The Story of Oscar
Written by Karen Koczwara

"Hey, kid. Get up! You can't sleep here."

Someone was kicking my feet. I rubbed my eyes grog-gily and slowly sat up. Two no-nonsense police officers stared down at me in disdain. "Sorry, I just …"

"We've seen the likes of you here before," one of the officers sneered, shining his flashlight directly into my eyes.

I squinted at the bright light and tried to stand. My legs were cramped from huddling in the fetal position all night. "All right, all right." I stood up and hung my head. For the first time, I noticed how filthy my shoes were, how my tattered jeans hung loosely on my slender frame and how terrible I smelled. I couldn't remember the last time I'd showered.

"No more sleeping in these halls, understand?" The other officer shoved his flashlight back in the holster. "What's a kid like you doing in these parts, anyhow?"

I shrugged. Truth was I didn't really know myself. I didn't put much thought into where I ended up. My life merely consisted of existing and surviving day after day, hour by hour. I stared after the two officers as they trudged out of the building and onto their next important mission. What did it matter to them if I slept here, any-way? This old hotel had been abandoned for years. I wasn't harming anyone. After all, as they'd pointed out themselves, I was just a kid.

I stepped outside and into the bright daylight, unsure of where to go next. My stomach growled loudly, reminding me that I hadn't eaten in two days. Time was a blur. I hadn't a clue of the day, of the week, or even the month. Shoving my dirty hands in my pockets, I headed down the street in search of my next meal. Hopefully the dumpsters would be generous today …

***

At just 4 years old, I had my first taste of death. My father, a hardworking man, passed away from cancer. Little was known about treating this terrible disease in the 1950s. My father succumbed to his illness on the couch in our tiny home in Spokane, Washington. I was scarcely old enough to understand what was going on, but I can still remember the great hole left in our lives after he passed away.

"It's best if children don't go to the funeral," my distraught mother explained quietly as she pulled on her best black dress. "You'll be looked after until I return."

Her eyes were sad and reddened, as if she'd been crying all night. I was too young to embrace the love story of two people who would never grow old together. My mother's parents, both Hungarian Jews, had arranged a marriage for her prior to meeting my father. My mother defied their arrangement and ran off with my father at the age of 18. My parents had two daughters close in age. When the youngest girl was 3, they decided to try once more for a boy, and I was born on May 16, 1954. Another son followed three years later. It seemed we were perfectly complete. That is, until we lost my father.

My mother struggled to provide for us after my father died. Money was not merely tight; it was nearly non-existent. We drank powdered milk and ate generous amounts of peanut butter, with the occasional brown sugar sandwich, things I actually grew quite accustomed to with time. My mother met another man months after my father passed away, and they married quickly. I believe she was afraid she could no longer provide for us on her own and wanted a caretaker to replace my father.

My stepfather was a stern man of few words. A former Navy aircraft carrier engineer, he had adapted a quiet coldness about him that carried into our home. Though he was only average in stature, my stepfather intimidated me. His wrath was not something anyone wanted to acquire.

One evening, my stepfather came home from work, kicked off his boots, sank onto the couch, opened his newspaper and turned on the TV news. This was his usual post-work routine, and we children knew better than to disturb him. I stepped into the room and quietly sat to the side of the TV, trying to get a glimpse of the program.

My stepfather looked up and, without saying a word, promptly picked up one of his boots and threw it at me. The look on his face said it all: I had crossed the line. I had invaded his territory, and he wasn't happy about it.

"Sorry, sir," I muttered, slinking out of the room.

On another occasion, I came home to find my stepfather chasing my older sister around our tiny house. My sister ran from the kitchen and back to the living room, a look of terror in her eyes. I stopped in my tracks and watched the scene unfold before me, knowing I had to do something to stop him.

On impulse, I kicked a kitchen chair out in my stepfather's path, causing him to trip and stumble. My sister escaped and ran out the back door, slamming it behind her. I followed quickly before I could catch a glimpse of my stepfather's snarl. He was known to yank off his belt and whip me with it. I wasn't in the mood for it that day.

One afternoon, a couple of young men showed up at our door. They spoke to my mother and stepfather for some time while I watched with growing curiosity from the kitchen.

"They were some nice missionaries from the Mormon church," my mother explained when the couple left, nodding toward a stack of literature in her hand. "They invited us to their church on Sunday. I think we'll go."

My stepfather had never been particularly interested in religious matters before, but my mother took us to Vacation Bible School one summer. I figured it couldn't hurt to go to church on Sunday, though. Lots of kids I knew went to Sunday school and seemed to like it okay.

When Sunday rolled around, I donned my best clothes and watched as my siblings pulled on their stockings and freshly pressed pants.

A PLACE TO CALL HOME

My mother turned to us as the car rumbled down the drive. "Remember, children, good manners. We're going to God's house to worship."

We nodded solemnly, unsure of what to expect. I tugged at my crisply starched shirt, wishing I could trade it for a comfortable t-shirt.

The Mormon church quickly became a large part of our lives over the next few years. We attended services on Sundays and Wednesdays, and on Thursdays, I attended Cub Scouts. I liked my Cub Scout master, Don, immensely. The program was a refreshing change from the regimented, formal services we attended.

When I was 8 years old, the age of accountability in the Mormon faith, I was baptized. The ritual meant nothing to me, but I went along with it all the same. Boys in the Mormon church did not question their elders; they merely followed suit.

Shortly after the baptism, my entire family was sealed in the temple. This was a Mormon ritual in which a family was brought together in a ceremony so that they might be together for eternity. Though the building was intricately designed, it seemed to bear a certain hollow emptiness. At this point, I was quite confused about the Mormon religion. Though we read the Bible some, along with the Book of Mormon, I had no real understanding of God. It would be years before I would understand how to have a true and meaningful relationship with him.

When I was a bit older, I went to my uncle's farm to stay with him for a while. He took me to a Baptist church one Sunday. It was quite unlike the regimented church I'd been attending.

After the pastor preached his message, he said, "If anyone would like to know Jesus and is just too timid to come to the altar, please come to my office after the service."

I nearly jumped out of my seat. I *did* want to know more about Jesus! I nearly raced to his office, where I told the pastor I wanted to know more about having a true relationship with Jesus.

"You can do that today, son," the pastor explained. "You just need to pray a simple prayer, asking him to forgive the wrong things you've done in your life and to come into your life and help you do right."

We kneeled down, and I prayed the prayer along with him, half expecting some sort of magical thrill to run through my body. When nothing happened, I looked up, rather disappointed. "Is that it?" I asked solemnly.

"Yup. That's it."

I stepped outside where my extended family was waiting for me. "Congratulations, Oscar!" They beamed. I was a bit baffled by their newfound cheeriness.

I was still confused. I had done what the pastor had told me to do, but I still didn't really understand it all. How could Jesus really be the Lord of my life?

One afternoon while riding my bike home with some friends, I accidentally rode into a neighbor's garden. My stepfather learned about the incident and grew angry.

"You're grounded, boy. You'll stay in the yard all summer and work hard for me, you hear? No going out with friends, no runnin' around the neighborhood gettin' into mischief." That was his idea of keeping me out of trouble, keeping me in the backyard.

If looks could kill, I would have dropped dead on the spot. I trudged off to my room, heaving a great sigh. It wasn't as if I had many friends, anyway. I was the smallest kid in my class and had always had trouble making friends. The few I did have weren't the sort my parents would have approved of me bringing home. It seemed to be shaping up to be a long, lonely summer.

Not long after this incident, I got in trouble for shoplifting. I got caught by the law and was sent to Juvenile Detention. When my stepfather learned of my plight, he refused to let me come back home.

"Boy, you're gonna spend the rest of your life in trouble if you don't get your head on straight," he snarled.

My mom spoke through tears. "Dad isn't going to allow you to come back home this time."

I was shocked. I knew my stepfather wasn't particularly fond of me, but I found it hard to believe he would actually turn me over to the detention center!

I soon realized just how serious my stepfather was. My mother, though a sweet, loving woman, usually succumbed to his ruling in the house. She was busy raising their new babies and had little time to devote to my antics. It looked as if I had been turned out for good.

I was sent to reform school for a couple of years and then to a foster home. The days were long, and the nights were lonely for a boy of 14. I often thought about my family at dinnertime, wondering if they sat around clanking their forks and chatting happily as though I'd never existed. My foster parents were nice enough, but they couldn't replace family.

One day, I met a man named Rudy who ran a traveling carnival. "You lookin' for a job, kid? I can take you on the road with me. You can stay on as long as you want, and if you ever decide you're done, I'll buy you a bus ticket home."

My eyes grew wide at the thought of traveling the country with a carnival. I figured I had nothing to lose. "Sure," I replied, shrugging. "Sounds exciting."

***

Rudy was retired from the Barnum and Bailey Circus where he had spent years as a high wire walker. He had a thick German accent and drank quite heavily, but I came to enjoy his company. He made me his right-hand man; I assisted with stage tear down and set up and helped him build new sets for his acts. It was always exciting to see what kind of crowd we might draw at each new location and how they would respond to our acts. One of the most popular illusions was a bathing suit-clad girl who disappeared into a cage and reappeared as a gorilla. It was really just a man in a gorilla costume, but when he tried to break free of the cage, the audience tried to run for their lives. I had seen it a hundred times, and it always gave me a good laugh.

A PLACE TO CALL HOME

One night after the show was over, Rudy approached me backstage. A man in a button-up silk shirt stood next to him. "This here is my brother-in-law, kid. See the nice clothes he wears? See that shiny Buick Riviera he's drivin' out there? Isn't that a nice car?"

I gulped and nodded. "Sure. It's a nice car all right."

Rudy wagged his finger at me. "You think that's all nice, but you don't want to work hard enough to ever get any of that, now do you?" He inched closer to me. "Do you, I said?" he sneered.

I took a step backward. *Why was he talking this way to me?* "I do, sir. I do work hard …" I stammered.

"No, you don't. You're nothin' but a lazy kid. That's all you are. Just tryin' to bum a free ride off of us."

"I'm not, sir; I promise!" I protested, growing angry. I paused for a moment, still trying to understand why he was turning on me. "You said the moment I wanted to leave this deal, you'd buy me a ticket home. Well, I'm done. I'm outta here."

Rudy rolled his eyes. "Whatever, kid. I don't need you."

I returned to Washington where I started roaming the streets. I was just 15 and uncertain of what to do next in my life. My parents hadn't bothered to look for me after turning me out.

I was fairly certain my stepfather was happy to have me out of his hair. Suddenly, it seemed no one wanted me. Maybe I was just better off on my own. I was a smart kid. I could take care of myself.

STRENGTH FOR TODAY

***

I met a guy on the streets who told me I could share his apartment with him. This "apartment" turned out to be nothing but a rundown hotel room on the bad side of town. I plunked down what little cash I had at the front desk and cracked the door to what would be my future quarters.

Instantly, a musty smell filled my nostrils as I stepped inside the tiny room. In one corner sat a small twin-size bed; on the other side of the room stood an ancient-looking refrigerator. I shuddered to think what might be growing inside of it. There was no stove, only a hot plate for cooking food. The community bathroom down the hall smelled even worse. I held my breath as I poked my head in the shower, which was covered with mold and stains. It was better than the street, I reasoned, and decided it would have to do for now.

"Pancakes are ready," my roommate announced one morning as I rubbed the sleep out of my eyes. The rickety mattress always left me with an aching back in the morning.

"Pancakes?" I shuffled across the room as the sweet aroma filled the air. I hadn't eaten in two days; I would have stuffed my shoe in my mouth if I could have.

"Potato pancakes." My roommate held one up proudly and took a big bite. "Those potato flakes come in handy for lots of things," he chuckled.

"Cool," I mumbled, taking one eagerly. It was thick

and rather tasteless, but at least it would stop the stomach pains for a few hours.

Eventually, the food boxes ran out, and I was forced back onto the streets. I quickly learned the way of the streets. It was all about survival. In the mornings, I went in search of a meal, which could come from a dumpster or from a local grocery store. I discovered it was quite easy to saunter into a store, stuff an apple and some lunchmeat into my shirt and slip out without paying. I also found out about a local farm where I picked eggplant and learned to live off of that for a few weeks. It wasn't exactly a meal fit for a king, but then, I wasn't living in a palace, either.

I learned of a local shelter, which housed children and adults alike. Each morning, a large bag of donuts would arrive at the shelter, along with steaming hot coffee. A set of comfortable couches and ping-pong tables served as a recreation room there. On-site counseling was also available. I popped in every now and then to check it out.

Around this time, I began drinking. It started with wine and led to my new favorite drink, Mogan David. Being in a flat bottle, it was easy to shoplift and was very potent stuff.

I'd been exposed to alcohol with Rudy and the carnival and had seen the way it made him forget about all his cares for a few hours. Forgetting about my cares seemed like a pretty nice thing to do. I also found that if I got drunk, I could fall asleep anywhere. This included gutters, parks and even behind dumpsters. A large garbage bag served as my blanket, a meager attempt to keep the biting cold from eating me alive overnight, though I woke up sweaty and stinking.

Drinking led to drugs, the next step for folks on the street. It was easy to get my hands on speed, the most popular street drug. I learned that if I used speed, I could stay up all night, which meant I didn't need to worry about sleeping arrangements. I spent my days wandering the streets or hanging out and napping at the local shelter. Life was going nowhere fast.

One day, I grew gravely ill. I could barely stand up and became confused and disoriented. A local prostitute named Cookie came to my side. "Hey, kid, come with me. You need something to eat," Cookie coaxed.

"Thanks," I muttered and followed her to a local restaurant. I could practically taste the food on my lips the moment I walked through the doors. I couldn't remember the last time I'd had a hot meal.

"Here, eat." Cookie shoved a plate of steaming hot food in front of me. "You look like s***, kid."

I stared at her, taking in worn features, which at one time must have been quite attractive. I didn't know much about Cookie, but the hollowness in her eyes told me she must have led a very hard life, too.

I stabbed the food and put a generous amount in my mouth, savoring every bite. For just a moment, I was back home, sitting around the table with my family, eating dinner and laughing. Then I promptly got sick and threw up on the carpet of the restaurant.

Cookie took care of me for the next week, feeding me

and giving me a place to stay. Then it was back to the streets. I headed straight for my next high. By now, I was doing speed intravenously and had contracted Hepatitis. Even this did not stop me from using drugs. They were now the only friend I had.

I met a guy at a local coffee shop. He agreed to let me sleep under his pool table at night in exchange for getting him drugs. I was happy to oblige. A hard floor indoors sure beat the cold back alley behind a smelly dumpster.

One day while hanging out at the local shelter, I looked up to see my brother walk through the door. He strode toward me with an uncertain look on his face. "Oscar?" he stammered.

I was surprised to see him and suddenly ashamed of my tattered clothes and long matted hair. "How'd you find me?"

He shrugged. "Figured this was where you'd end up. You okay? You don't look so great."

"I'm fine," I replied quickly. "Just takin' it day by day. Yourself?"

"Fine. Everything's fine." He looked uncomfortable as he scanned the room, his eyes taking in the couple of scroungy-looking guys at the pool table. "Well, I better, uh, get going. I'll tell everyone hello for you. All right?"

I nodded. "Sure. You do that." I bummed five dollars from him and watched him go, a certain anger welling inside of me. How could my stepfather not care? How could life go on just miles from here while I wandered the streets of Skid Row?

One day, I stumbled into a local coffee shop. A group of hippie guys, whom we street people called "Jesus Freaks," were playing in a band. Each time a person entered the shop, they looked up, waved and called out, "Jesus loves you, man!"

This group of guys fascinated me. I had grown up hearing about God and doing good things in the Mormon church but still never really understood how to have a real and meaningful relationship with Jesus. These guys seemed happy enough. Did they have that relationship? As curious as I was, I never stepped forward to ask more.

I spent the next couple of years wandering the streets, often hitchhiking for something to do. I learned that if I could catch a ride somewhere, I could sleep for hours in the car.

"Where to, kid?" A man in a pickup truck pulled up to the curb one rainy night.

"Anywhere you're goin'," I replied.

"California."

I shrugged. "Sure. I've got no place to go." I hopped in and leaned back against the seat. Sometimes I was in the mood for conversation, but most times, I was just happy to have a place to rest my head for a few days.

"Hungry?" The man pulled out a sandwich from a paper bag and handed it to me.

"Thanks," I replied. I tried not to gobble it too quickly. If he only knew this was the first meal I'd had in two days!

When hitchhiking grew boring, I began stealing cars to joyride in. I was surprised at how many people left their keys in their cars. One particular evening, my little jaunt nearly cost me my life.

While joyriding around in a 1954 pickup truck, I spotted a highway patrol car in the other lane of the road. I spun a quick u-turn from the far right lane I was in but didn't check my rearview mirrors and was slammed into by a large truck. I obtained a severe skull fracture that should have easily killed me.

"You're lucky to be alive," the doctor declared as I regained consciousness. "That was one nasty accident."

Indeed, I was lucky to be alive, but even that didn't shake me to the point of quitting my mischief. One night in the fall of 1971, I decided to steal a car and drive to the outskirts of town. I'd gone no more than 100 or so miles when a cop pulled me over. He soon discovered I was driving a stolen car without a license. I was sentenced to jail and probation. Because it was so close to my 18th birthday, I was sentenced as an adult but sent to a Mormon foster home.

Instead of learning from my mistakes, I turned right back around and headed for more trouble. Drinking and drugs were the only two friends I knew. I went joyriding with an old acquaintance from the street, this time taking a car to the highways of Montana. It was here I was caught for good and taken to prison as an adult.

The first day I arrived at the prison, I was horrified to see an older man stabbed to death by three guys. The blood on the floor was so deep that my shoes left red sticky footprints all the way to my cell. I was quite shaken by the violence inside these walls and prayed no harm would come to me.

I was given a job in the prison kitchen where a guy began harassing me regularly. "You gonna be my b****, man," he sneered at me over and over.

At last, I stood up to him, but he retaliated by pulling out a homemade knife and trying to stab me! Thankfully, I'd spent three years doing martial arts training when I was a kid.

I defended myself as the angry knife-wielding guy came at me. He managed to stab me in the arm, but I spun around just in time to keep the knife from penetrating my heart. I then made a run for the infirmary upstairs.

Halfway up the stairs, a few other guys jumped out to attack me. Heart racing, I managed to escape to the infirmary where I was stitched up. Once again, God had protected me from what could have been a deadly encounter.

During the summer of 1976, I was furloughed for a week. I hopped on a plane and flew to Seattle. When I arrived, I began wandering the street, hoping to catch a glimpse of the famous Space Needle building. I had obtained some social security money from my late father while in prison and had quickly blown it on drugs. I had a hefty amount of marijuana on me.

I spotted an attractive girl sitting near the street, looking deep in thought. Something about her smile made me stop in my tracks. "Hey, there. You want to smoke?" I flashed her my pipe inside my jacket.

"Sure." She stood up and followed me to the park.

"I'm Oscar," I told her as we shuffled down the side-walk. "And you?"

"Jean. You live around here?"

I paused. "Sort of. You?"

"I live up north a bit. Just here visiting."

Jean and I were inseparable for the next week. I en-joyed her company immensely. She was smart, funny and quite good-looking. It seemed we had everything in com-mon. We became intimate one night. I felt it was justified as I had never loved a woman like I had Jean. I never wanted to leave her.

I failed to return to prison but was caught and trans-ferred to one of the largest state penitentiaries on the West Coast. Life inside the prison walls was rough. The correc-tional officers didn't really care what people did, so long as they didn't escape. I did my best to keep to myself and tried to stay out of trouble for the two years I spent there. While I did visit the prison chapel a few times, the services left little impression on me. I was still very much confused and did not understand how to have a true relationship with God.

One evening shortly after being transferred there, Jean paid me a surprise visit.

"Jean, what are you doing here?" I asked, not bother-ing to hide my enthusiasm. "I thought I'd never see you again!"

"I'm pregnant, Oscar. I was raped," she replied quietly.

"Oh, wow." I didn't know what to say.

"I'll help you take care of the child. You're not alone in

this," I replied. I was excited that Jean and I were going to raise a baby. Now we had something to bond us for life!

I signed paternity papers when the child was born, but to my chagrin, Jean stopped contacting me shortly after that. I soon learned that our son was the result of an affair, not a rape as I was led to believe. I couldn't blame her; how could a guy who bounced between prison and the streets provide for a child?

Toward the end of my sentence, I was sent to Forest Camp where inmates nearing the end of their time were taught to fight fires. One evening, a group of buddies sent me to buy wine in town. I thought it was only a mile or two to town from the fire camp, but it turned out to be several miles to the nearest store. On a whim, I kept on traveling.

While walking through a small downtown, I saw a cop pass me and impulsively flipped him off. Several minutes later, another cop passed me, and I flipped him off as well. My little game turned out to be a bust, though. I had flipped off the same cop twice!

"Tryin' to be funny, huh?" the cop muttered as he took me into his custody. "Game over, kid."

Game over, indeed! I was sent back to prison for the next four years. At last, in the summer of 1983, I was paroled from prison. I learned about a tiny town called Culp Creek where many families from Kentucky had come out to log and stake their claim on gold. With nowhere to go and nothing to lose, I decided to move there and see if I could get my hands on some of this gold.

A PLACE TO CALL HOME

For just a few dollars, I could stake a claim with the county for a 20-acre plot of land. While it was not technically private property, I would have the liberty to live on this mountain land and mine on it for as long as I liked. It seemed too good to be true!

I set up a tent on the land and spent the next several weeks sleeping with my dog in a thin castoff sleeping bag at night. During the day, I spent hours sifting through the ice-cold water in the nearby creek in hopes of finding a few precious pieces of gold. At the end of the week, I made the 17-mile hike down the mountain into the little town. Once there, I tried to exchange my gold for groceries and basic essentials. Along the way, I also picked up cans, which I turned in for cash to buy bread, peanut butter, beans and, of course, beer.

Culp Creek was a town of 300 people. An old logging town, it boasted only one general store with a couple of gas pumps out front. I became friendly with the locals and got to know them on a first-name basis.

"Hey, I got a trailer I ain't usin'," a man told me one day. "You want it?"

"Sure." Anything beat sleeping in an old worn tent.

An old 1952 aluminum trailer became my home for the next couple of years. Five feet by 8 feet in dimension, it was just large enough to serve as a living room, kitchen and bedroom, all in one. With a kerosene light and little woodstove, my living expenses were minimal, and grouse, fish and deer were always in season. I continued mining and drinking beer around a campfire at night. It was a lonely but simple life, and for a while, I thought I was okay.

I met a nice family in town who offered to help me build a cabin up on my property. Shortly after the cabin was completed, I attended a church service where I met a man named Trent. Trent traveled as a roadie for missionaries who performed feats of strength at local schools.

"You should come with me and check it out sometime," Trent insisted. "The schools won't let us talk about God, but the kids are real impressed when we break out of metal handcuffs and blow up water bottles. After the show is over, we get a chance to invite them to church."

Life on the mountain had grown lonely, and I decided traveling around with Trent might be a nice change of pace. We became friends, and I went on to be a roadie with him, traveling from school to school. As we traveled, Trent sometimes talked about Jesus and how much he loved him. Though I had attended church off and on over the years, I hadn't really given much thought to God for some time. I enjoyed my conversations with Trent; they stirred up questions I'd been dealing with for years. Who was God, really, and what did it mean to have a true relationship with him? I thought perhaps Trent had all the answers, but it turned out he was every bit as confused as I was.

"I can't live anymore, man," Trent confessed to me one night as we hopped in the car after a show. "I think I'm gonna kill myself."

"What are you talking about?" I retorted.

"I just can't go on. Life sucks," Trent muttered.

I soon learned Trent suffered from manic depression, often going from periods of high intensity to terrible lows. During these lows, he became suicidal, and I grew afraid. I eventually decided it was best to part ways with Trent and returned to the mountains to continue mining.

I'd thought I'd enjoy the quiet peace of the mountains, but instead, loneliness overwhelmed me. For years, I'd told myself that being alone did not necessarily mean I was lonely. But now, I knew this was false. I grew tired of staring up at the sky each night, counting stars and drinking beer alone. As the days passed, I thought more and more about God. I wanted to know him, really know him, but just didn't know how. He seemed so distant, so far off. How could the God of the universe want anything to do with a messed up, wayward guy like me?

One night as the fire crackled beside me, sending a warm glow up toward the sky, I stood to my feet, shook my fists upward and yelled at the top of my lungs, "Show me! Show me you're real, God! Strike me blind as you did to Saul!" I'd read the story of Saul in the Bible, a man who'd done terrible things but had been struck blind by God. Saul had then turned into Paul and had gone on to do great things for the Lord. I didn't truly want to go blind, but I did want to encounter God in a powerful and real way. *Where was he? Did he even hear me? And would I ever find purpose to my seemingly meaningless life?*

At last, I could take the loneliness no longer. What had once seemed exciting now seemed terribly empty. Eight years after I first set up the tent on my land, I retreated down the mountain. I soon met a man who sold and installed satellite dishes. I agreed to help him with his business. I found a small house to rent for $200 a month, which I could now easily afford with my "real" job.

Each afternoon, I walked to the post office down a certain road. I always passed a house where a woman stood outside gardening. Something about her quiet smile intrigued me.

"I really enjoy seeing your garden," I called out, stopping to admire her new flowers.

"Thank you," she replied warmly. "Guess God's blessed me with a green thumb." She chuckled. "I see you walking this way every day. You must live nearby?"

I nodded down the street. "Yup, just up a ways. I'm Oscar." I scanned her face, guessing her to be in her early 40s. Her eyes were warm, and her smile genuine.

"I'm Corliss," she replied. "Nice to meet you."

Corliss and I continued to talk each day as I passed her house, and a deep friendship blossomed from our conversations. I learned that Corliss was a Christian and had a deep faith in the Lord. Eventually, Corliss invited me to attend church with her. I agreed to go.

The tiny church Corliss attended was unlike anything I'd ever experienced. I was not completely comfortable with the setting but kept going week after week. Meanwhile, a romance grew between us. One day, I asked her to marry me.

"Of course I'll marry you, Oscar!" Corliss beamed.

A PLACE TO CALL HOME

Corliss and I married in August of 1996, the hottest day of the entire year. Corliss had six children of her own, including three who were already grown. I knew it would be a challenge stepping into their lives as a father figure, but at the same time, I was eager for the task. I also knew it was time to find myself a "real" job to support my new family.

I went to a local temp agency, which immediately found me work at the University of Oregon upgrading phone, data and television lines. They hired me permanently after two weeks. From there, I went on to work in many areas of telecommunications. Despite lacking a professional degree, the Lord blessed me in ways I never thought possible.

In August of 2001, a larger company bought the one I was working for, and we were required to relocate to Madras, Oregon. Corliss and I found a beautiful manufactured home on an acre of land. It was nothing more than a large patch of weeds to begin with, but within a few years, Corliss had worked her magic green thumb, and beauty surrounded us!

Meanwhile, one of our granddaughters came to live with us. She attended a youth group at a nearby church each week. She often got home after 9 p.m., excited about what she'd experienced.

"Tell me more about this place you can't stop talking about," I encouraged her, curious. *What kind of place is keeping my granddaughter up so late?*

"Oh, it's great!" she gushed. "It's called Living Hope

Christian Center. The pastors and people are all really welcoming, and I'm learning so much about God. You really should check it out."

Corliss and I fell in love with Living Hope Christian Center. Just as our granddaughter had said, it was full of kind, compassionate people who welcomed us right away. Pastor Lee was a genuine man who preached a solid message from the Bible. It took some time for me to get accustomed to raising my hands while singing during worship, but eventually, I became comfortable with this style of worship.

For the first time, I felt I was developing a genuine relationship with God. Pastor Lee spoke in simple terms that helped me understand things. The more I read my Bible, prayed and attended church, the more I learned who God really was. He was not a foreign figure up in the sky but rather a loving God who wanted to know me as a father does.

Though I enjoyed attending church and learning more about God, I still kept one foot in the world. I often stopped at the local bars on my motorcycle after a long day's work. I hoped I wouldn't run into anyone from church outside the bar, as I feared he or she might not approve.

As the years passed, Corliss and I grew more involved with our church and enjoyed meeting new people who encouraged us in our faith. I continued to learn more and more about the Lord yet still desired to be filled with his presence in a more tangible way.

"Lord, please show yourself to me," I prayed as I had on the mountain. "Please make yourself very real to me!"

In April 2007, more than five years after we first began attending Living Hope, I found myself seated in church as I did every Sunday. As Pastor Lee's wife began to lead worship and fill the sanctuary with her beautiful voice, I felt the overwhelming presence of the Lord come over me. It was unlike anything I'd ever experienced in my life. Suddenly, for a moment, I was in the lap of God as he held me close, soaked in his unfailing love. I collapsed in awe in my seat as the church continued to sing. I had felt every drug high this world could offer. I had chased every chemical rush known to man. God's presence outshined anything I could ever imagine. I was undone by just one moment with God.

"Thank you, Lord," I whispered as tears filled my eyes. "Thank you for showing yourself to me." The prayer I had prayed over and over as a lonely mountain man had finally been answered. The Lord had met with me, an extraordinary moment on a very ordinary Sunday morning.

Two weeks later, I had another amazing encounter with God while sitting in church. As I sat taking in the worship, I found Jesus holding my hand. "Was it worth it?" I whispered, referring to the great sacrifice he had paid by dying on the cross for me. "Was it worth it, Jesus?"

"Yes, it was," I heard him say with a smile. "Yes, it was."

Again, a great warmth surged through my soul. Jesus was very real in my life! He loved me, just as I was. He was pleased with me, despite my wretched self. I felt at that moment that I could fly to the skies and back, proclaiming the goodness of God. "Thank you," I whispered quietly. "Thank you."

That next month, I was baptized in front of my entire church. It was a wonderful feeling to proclaim my love for Jesus in front of my fellow church members. I no longer wanted to be a closet Christian, going to bars during the week and church on Sunday. I wanted to live my life every day for Christ.

"I bought you a new Bible," Corliss said to me one day, presenting me with a beautiful New King James Study Bible. "I hope you like it."

Tears sprang to my eyes as I turned the soft leather book over and over in my hands. For the first time, I had a true desire to devour God's word. I immediately began to pore over it, amazed at how God spoke to me through the scriptures. The book of Romans became a fast favorite of mine. I loved the way the author, Paul, talked about struggling against his fleshly desires to do wrong. Paul was a very godly man, yet even he struggled with sin! I wanted to surrender my life to Christ as he did, living each day under God's amazing grace.

Slowly, God began to heal the other wounds in my life. I re-established a relationship with my mother and learned to forgive my stepfather for his ways.

I also got in touch with my son, Dustin, via the Internet, and learned he had just gotten married. I had spent years wondering what happened to him and could now rejoice knowing God had brought our paths together.

Meanwhile, my life with Corliss and the children continued to thrive. We loved pouring ourselves into our family and teaching them about God. We continued to grow in our relationship with God at Living Hope, while my career in telecommunications also blossomed.

"God, you've been so good to me. You've given me more than I could have dreamed of," I prayed one night as I flipped my Bible shut. "You've given me a beautiful wife, children, a wonderful church, a fulfilling job and, most importantly, a true relationship with you. I finally feel that I have purpose in my life!"

As I prayed, I thought about the man I'd once been, wandering the streets, stealing cars, living a lonely mountain life. I'd once only existed to survive, while I now existed to thrive! God had truly shown himself to me. He was good!

***

"Terrible news, Oscar. Jessie's been killed." Corliss could hardly speak as she hung up the phone and sunk onto the couch.

My heart raced wildly. "Killed?" I croaked. Jessie, our precious 6-year-old granddaughter, killed?!

We soon learned Jessie had been run over by a bulldozer the day before. It was a terrible, tragic accident that left everyone in the community reeling. Though our family grieved her terribly, we clung to the Lord like we never had before. Our church family surrounded us with prayer, which we coveted.

A few days after Jessie's tragic death, I learned of something that would impact me forever. Immediately following the accident, Jessie's mother, along with her aunt, ran to the young child and scooped Jessie into her arms. Instead of shaking her fist at God for taking her daughter, she instead began to sing praises to him! Despite her aching heart, she thanked God for the precious time she'd been able to spend with her daughter on earth and praised him for taking Jessie to be with him in heaven.

To most, this would seem unfathomable. How could she not be angry with God? Did she not grieve? Yes, she most certainly did grieve as any distraught parent would over the death of a child. But she had grasped the great power of a loving God and knew that despite her pain, he still cared. Years of instilling the power of God's word in our children at home had not been in vain.

Though my heart ached over this terrible loss, I, too, found hope in the Lord. He had proven himself real to me, and I knew that even in the midst of our sorrow, he had not failed us. He was good, always. He had blessed me with a home after years of not knowing where I'd sleep. But Jessie had found the best home of all. She was now in the arms of Jesus. And one day, I would be, too.

DADDY'S LITTLE GIRL
THE STORY OF BONNIE
WRITTEN BY CONNIE RUTH CHRISTIANSEN

My 4-year-old heart just barely ventured to consider happiness as I pictured the strong dark form of my father striding down the driveway and up to the front door. He was grinning from ear to ear with shining perfect white teeth. He walked with a lilt in his step because he was so excited to finally be reunited with his long-lost little girl. He was coming to take me away from this place of sadness, away from this house where everyone had pale hair and skin, except for me, away from these people who called me "bastard child." I didn't know what that meant, but I knew by the tone in their voices that it was not good. My daddy was coming for me! He had found me! He had been looking for me for a very long time, and now Daddy was finally coming to take me to my real home!

"Dad's home, Bonnie. Dad's home," an unwelcome voice whispered behind me, shattering my hopeful fantasy. I turned to see my siblings, all stealing away from the living room toward the back of our house, and I quickly joined them. The five of us made it a point to avoid meeting Dad when he strode in from work so as to escape being caught in the fire of his forever-angry words.

Mom, who loved to sing and play and giggle with her children throughout the day, would grow silent in the evening, cowering from her husband's abusive remarks. At the evening meal, we would sit rigidly around the table, ever watchful to not tip over the milk or drop food from the fork to the floor or the table. When Dad was home, we were miserable.

When I was still too young to understand, I found out that Dad wasn't my real father. My unhappy mother had fallen in love with a married man, and I was the result of their union. My stepfather made no secret of the fact that he despised the child who was a constant reminder of his wife's unfaithfulness. I tried desperately to win his approval, to no avail. I wondered what I had done wrong. Perhaps if I were blond, he would love me more or at least hate me less. I would escape often to my world of make believe and to that oh-so-wonderful day when my real father, my daddy, would sweep in and take me away to live happily ever after. My daddy never came.

My mother met my biological father at a place and time shrouded in mystery. She was looking for something to fill the void of a loveless marriage, and so she began attending meetings in a neighbor's basement room. There she was, drawn into a seductive spiritual underworld and began to take part in rituals she would not speak of. My sisters tell a story of sneaking down the basement stairs into that dark secret room where, to their horror, they saw what looked like a human baby being sacrificed upon a bloody altar. As incredible as it may seem, they are still convinced of what they saw, all these years later.

My stepfather told me a related story. When Mom was almost nine months pregnant with me, he heard screaming coming from their bedroom and Mom crying out for God to help her. He ran down the hall to the room but could not open the door. There was no lock on the door, but it felt to him as if something was preventing him from entering. When the door finally gave way to his pounding and pushing, Dad found my mother cowering upon the bed, terrified. She told him over and over that demonic forces had been surrounding the bed, clawing at her full belly, trying to get to the baby.

After my birth, my mother's mental state continued to deteriorate. She was eventually diagnosed as a paranoid schizophrenic. In spite of her illness, she was the one bright spot in my young life. I didn't understand some of the bizarre things she said and did, but she was my mommy, and I adored her. Mommy depended on me, and I felt responsible for her; that was a good feeling. My siblings were overtly jealous of the exceptional bond between our mother and me, and most of the kids in the neighborhood were not allowed to play with me because of my close connection to the "crazy lady." In my sad world, even the love my parent had for me was turned into rejection by those who did not understand.

When I was 5 years old, my stepfather, siblings and I piled in the car for an outing. We were going to visit Mom at the mental hospital. Along the way, we stopped at a photographer's studio. Dad wanted a photo to send to his family. How excited we all were! And then, he told me I was not to be a part of that picture — just him and his fair-haired children. Tears welled in my small eyelids as my heart broke. Two of my sisters responded to my tears by crying, also, and by telling Dad they would not be a part of the picture unless I was. They angrily stood their ground until he gave in. "Get your g*d d**n butt over here!" he said as he gruffly pulled me into the picture.

I still have a copy of that photograph. There stands my stepfather, surrounded by his smiling blond children, all dressed in their Sunday best. And there I stand, off to one side, my clothing rumpled, my dark hair a mess, my face stained with tears.

When Mom was home from the hospital, she would sometimes get up in the middle of the night to go on long walks to nowhere in particular. I would climb out of bed and follow close behind. She did her best to hide her trail or to walk in various patterns so as to throw "them" off. There were so many times my little legs were barely able to keep up, but on she would go, and so would I. I felt like I *had* to protect her.

When I was 6 years old, one of our midnight jaunts took us clear across town to a Chinese restaurant. As we were leaving, a truck with three men pulled alongside us to ask if we needed a ride. I knew something wasn't right, and I was determined we should not get into the truck with them. I don't know what happened next. The next thing I remember, I was walking alone by the side of the road in my soiled bright pink jumpsuit with rainbow suspenders, about a mile from our home.

A cop car pulled up next to me, and a kindhearted policeman called out through an open window to ask if I was

Bonnie Campbell. I nodded my head yes and kept right on walking.

He climbed out of the car and said, "Climb in, and I'll take you to your mom."

"I can't. I peed all down the legs of my pants," I answered, embarrassed.

At that point, this gentle giant in uniform picked me up, wrapped his big strong arms around me and wept openly. I had never been held in a man's arms before. I still remember the smell of his cologne, which I later learned was the smell of Old Spice.

Starving for love, acceptance and male attention, I married at the young age of 13. I manipulated my mother into signing consent for the marriage by threatening to never see her again or committing suicide. My husband, Mike, was six years older than me and treated me the only way he knew how, the way his father had treated his mother — he beat me often. After the rage was over, he would cry and tell me he was sorry and that it would never happen again. He would gently pull me to him and hold me, caress me, tell me that he loved me. This passive-aggressive attention was the closest thing to love I had ever experienced. For those measly breadcrumbs of intimacy, I endured the pain, and I stayed.

When I was pregnant with our first child, Mike beat me so brutally that I lost the baby. Afraid for my own life, I escaped to his grandparents' home. He followed me there, broke in and raped me. The result of that assault was another pregnancy. Eventually, I returned home to

Mike where things were quiet between us for a time. I was four months pregnant when he once again grew angry enough to beat me with the intent of killing our second child. Thankfully, he did not succeed in ending another life. He did succeed, however, in convincing me to finally leave him.

Having nowhere else to go, I went to the home of my stepfather who, much to my surprise, welcomed me in and was very supportive of my pregnancy and plight. Five months later, I gave birth to a beautiful baby girl.

It wasn't long before I was once more looking for that ever-elusive thing called love. My journey led me to Clyde, who was attentive and seemed to want to take care of me and my daughter. He further endeared himself to me by encouraging me to quit smoking marijuana, to which Mike had introduced me. Although I had told myself I would never trust another man to be my husband, at the age of 17, with hope in my heart, I said "I do" once again.

Clyde had a good job and worked very hard to take care of his new family. Over the course of three years, we had three babies. Life was good. And then, we decided to move across the country, away from Mississippi to even greener pastures. As we settled into our new life in Arizona, my husband changed before my eyes. He began drinking heavily and pulling away from me emotionally. At home, we argued constantly, and in public, he treated me with disgust and disrespect. It was as if he was an entirely different person, as if he no longer loved me. Angry that once again I was being abandoned, I returned to smoking marijuana, experimenting with other drugs, drinking and partying — anything to fill the emptiness and numb the pain.

After about a year of both doing our own thing, I confronted Clyde and told him that if things didn't change, I was going to leave him. We decided to move again. It had always been a dream of his to move back to the state of his birth, and so we packed up and headed off for Madras, Oregon. Unfortunately, in spite of trying desperately for a fresh new start, our marriage struggles, his drinking and my drug problem escalated.

The drugs weren't taking the pain away; the booze wasn't filling the void. I was so tired! I had been rejected and abused by so many for so long, I just couldn't handle it any longer. My frustration fanned the embers of bitterness that smoldered deep within until rage burst into flame. I became consumed with anger, intent on vengeance. I would not be hurt again! I would hurt "them" first before "they" had a chance to take advantage of me. Men became the target of my fury; Clyde would feel my wrath.

One fateful day, Clyde took the boys and left for a motel. I retaliated by lying to the authorities and telling them that he had been abusive and had kidnapped the kids. The police stormed into his motel room to rescue the children, drag my husband off to jail and file a restraining order. This experience pushed Clyde to the edge of emotional stability. A few days later, he holed himself up in the motel room with a gun, threatening to commit suicide.

Clyde's brother asked for my help to talk him out of

ending his life. I somehow was able to convince him that suicide was not the answer to our marriage problems and that his kids needed him. Thankfully, he put down the gun and then reluctantly agreed that we should live apart.

A short time after we separated, Clyde's brother told me that my husband had been going to church. My response was bitter and cynical. I laughed and said, "God better help him; he's the only one who can!"

At Living Hope Christian Center, Clyde found a sliver of hope and a compassionate listening ear. He poured out the tale of his marriage troubles to the pastor, who then offered to give me a call. Clyde's response was less than hopeful. "You can, but it won't do any good. The marriage is over." Pastor Lee called me, anyway.

I did agree to a meeting with the pastor and Clyde, but not for the purpose of reconciliation. I was bent on vindication for the many wrongs done to me. I had to make known all of Clyde's inadequacies as a husband and tell of my virtues as wife and mother.

During the course of our three-way conversation, the pastor listened intently to my words. I did not listen much to what he had to say. One particular statement, however, grabbed a hold of me with such intense force that it almost knocked the wind out of me. Pastor Lee turned to me and said, "Bonnie, God knows you want the *Leave it to Beaver* life. He loves you, and he hears the deepest cry of your heart."

My mind started racing with questions. *How can he know? Who told him about the many times I had watched*

Leave it to Beaver *and longed for that life to be mine?* I had never told anyone how often I wished to enter that TV world with the loving mom, dad, dog and brother. *This is not a coincidence,* I thought. *This is* more *than a coincidence!*

That seemingly insignificant but very powerful statement about a television sitcom had weakened my defenses. Hope stirred within me. Perhaps God really did care about me. Perhaps there was a better life for me, for us. Before our time together was over that day, December 12, 1992, Clyde and I both prayed for God's help and forgiveness. We made a good-faith commitment to trust God and to give our marriage another try.

As we were getting ready to head home, Pastor Lee spoke a word of warning. "Now that you have decided to give God a place in your life, the devil is not about to just give up on you. Don't be surprised if things start going very wrong." And sure enough, as soon as Clyde and I and our newfound faith walked out of the church building onto the streets of the small town where everyone knew everyone else's business, a police car cruised by. The officer recognized us, stopped his car and got out. He walked over to Clyde and took him off to jail for violating the restraining order that had been filed due to the "motel incident."

Instead of heeding the pastor's warning about the devil's sly tactics, I began to doubt and question the validity of God's love for me. I did my best to convince myself that Pastor Lee had somehow found out about my *Leave it* to *Beaver* daydreams, and he had tricked me into accepting Jesus as my Savior. I thought, *This is all a bunch of crap! There's no way I am going to become some sort of Bible thumper!* The trouble was something had happened deep inside me when I prayed that prayer in Pastor Lee's office. I didn't understand it, but I couldn't quite convince myself it had been an illusion. Even my old faithful friend, the street drug, was unable to drown out the sound of truth that insisted on ringing in my ears and heart.

A few miserable days later, the evening of December 16, 1992, I found my way to the home of Pastor Lee. He and his wife, Cindy, welcomed me in and then stayed with me for hours, praying against all the doubts and fears and evil in my life. Well into the next morning, I mourned the lost joy and innocence of my childhood; I wept away the many years of abandonment and anger; I turned my disappointing existence over to Jesus. When the long night finally came to an exhausting end, I felt like a brand new person, like the chains of my painful past had been cut loose, like a huge weight had been lifted off my shoulders. I was free! I would never be the same from that day forward.

The next couple of years were a mixture of joy and frustration: the joy of learning about God's love, the frustration of learning to apply the principles of a newfound faith to our marriage. Clyde and I had to learn new ways of relating to one another. We had to learn to love and forgive, even when we didn't feel like loving or forgiving. Breaking old habits and replacing them with new ones is very hard work! I am reluctant to admit how many times I retreated into my overactive imagination to escape from the realities of that hard work. I imagined Clyde sitting me down and telling me that he was not going to try any longer, that it was just too hard and that he was leaving me for good. I also imagined him getting into a tragic accident. Clyde would die, everyone would feel sorry for me and the kids, the funeral would be wonderfully moving and I would be rid of the misery of trying to make a bad marriage better.

And then early one unforgettable morning, everything changed. Yawning and stretching the slumber out of my body, I turned over in bed to face my husband. As I gazed into his peaceful sleeping face, I was unexpectedly overwhelmed by an almost-familiar feeling. Was that love? It *was* love! I was *in love* with my husband! The eyes of my understanding became wide open to see how this man, with all his faults, truly did care about me and did his best to show me love on a regular basis.

What an incredible gift I had been given in this man! He was a good husband and a wonderful father. Watching my children with their daddy, I was overwhelmed with gratitude. What a wonderful, happy childhood they had. Their daddy adored them, protected them, held them, encouraged them, loved them. We had such fun as a family doing all the things I never did as a kid: camping and hiking, snowboarding and skiing, swimming and fishing. The joy of my children's lives began to color the memories of my past.

Going back through time, I began to see glimpses of my heavenly father's love, here and there, in my mother's care for me, in the tears and touch of a kind policeman, in my grade school teacher who used to whisper in my ear I was special and Jesus loved me. I began to see the love of God peeking out at me from everywhere and everything — in the colors of a rainbow, the glory of a sunset, the intricacies of a flower, the thunder of ocean waves.

There is a drawing by my nephew, Donnie, which describes how I felt as a child. It is a black and white portrayal of a small closet, consisting of one empty shelf. A bare light bulb hangs wobbly from the center of a cracked ceiling, giving out just enough light to see the dust and shadows. The only item, sitting awkwardly on the edge of the shelf, is a tiny, raggedy slumped-over doll. Her wide-open eyes are deep, dark pools of loneliness; her mouth turns downward at the corners as if she is about to burst into tears. Nailed above the opening to this closet of emptiness is a crooked, rugged sign, which reads "Forgotten." My life used to be that closet. I was that doll.

How different my life has become since that day in 1992 when I ventured to take a chance to trust that maybe, just maybe, God really did love me! That lonely, ragged doll has been picked up, dusted off and given a brand new home. My home is now my sanctuary, and over the years, it has become a shelter to more than 90 foster children. My husband loves and respects me. The pastor and his wife accept me as a precious child of God, just as I am. I have girlfriends that care about me as my siblings never knew how to. I even developed a close friendship with my stepfather, which lasted until his death. He died on the anniversary of my mother's birthday, and we buried him on Valentine's Day — both dates were reminders from my heavenly father that I am not forgotten.

Even on days when I *feel* lost, I am not forgotten. When circumstances of life tempt me to once again think of myself as a bastard child, when the unkind actions and words of people reopen the heart wounds of my past, I am so thankful for a heavenly father that cares about my pain, and I run to him for comfort.

Now, in my mind's eye, the little girl hiding away in her fantasy hopes for a daddy who never came has been transformed into a joyful child, dressed in a ballerina gown with long full sleeves that flutter as I twirl on my tippy-toes across a stage, bright with light. No one else is on the stage vying for time. It's just me dancing before my father in heaven, who smiles as he watches me, delights in me, is proud of me.

I am no longer the out-of-place one, shoved off to the side to make room for the "real" children in the photograph. I am the absolute center of God's attention. It was him I was searching for all along. And he was searching for me, his lost little one. He loves me! He *wants* me! I am his "real" child. I am my daddy's little girl.

SAFE ARMS
The Story of Bethany
Written by Karen Koczwara

Oh, my God. My heart sank as I opened the truck door. *Oh, God, no! This isn't my little boy. God, tell me this didn't just happen.*

"What happened, Al?" I croaked, not even sure the words had escaped my mouth.

"We were just wrestlin' around on the bed, and he fell off and hit his head on the closet door. He's okay," Al replied, shrugging.

Okay? My son was anything but okay. His eyes were completely swollen and filled with blood. The rest of his face was covered with dark bruises and scratch marks, as though a large animal had attacked him. My stomach twisted at the sight, and it was all I could do to keep from lunging at Al. *You did this! You monster! You hurt my son!*

"It was an accident, Mom," my son insisted. "I'm okay."

His tiny voice broke my heart. I took a deep breath and tried to maintain my composure. I would not, could not, lose it in front of him. "Um, honey, why don't you run off to the church now so I can talk to Daddy for a minute, okay?" I said in the calmest voice I could muster.

"Okay, Mom." He climbed out of the truck and scampered off — my brave, innocent boy.

Unfair, unfair, my heart screamed. How could this happen again?

***

"Where is Anna going?" I asked my mother, cowering by the bedroom door as I watched my older sister pack.

"Your sister's going away for a while," my mother replied quietly, ushering me down the hall. "Now be a good girl and get ready for church, all right?"

Confused, I returned to my room where I put on my best Sunday dress. I knew my 13-year-old sister, Anna, had gotten into a bit of trouble during the past couple of years, but I didn't realize things had gotten that serious.

I was born in Prince George's County, Maryland, on June 9, 1979. My parents divorced when I was 2, leaving me with virtually no memories of my father. My mother raised my two older sisters and me on her own. My oldest sister, Lisa, was the strong and stable one, often taking on the motherly role in our home. My middle sister, Anna, was the troublemaker. I was too young to understand that she was being sent off to rehab because she had gotten mixed up with drugs and the wrong crowd.

We attended Catholic church each Sunday, which I didn't much enjoy. My grandparents were Roman Catholic, and it was assumed our family would continue in their ways. The priest often talked about going to hell if we did bad things but never spoke about having a real relationship with Jesus. Religion seemed like a scary practice full of rules that, in our home, had already been broken.

My mother worked full-time and attended school at night. She struggled to make ends meet as a single parent. Still reeling from the divorce, my mother threw herself into many meaningless relationships with other men. Sometimes at night, I heard her having sex in the other room with her various visitors. I tried to cover my head with a pillow to block out the noise.

Junior high came all too soon for me. I struggled to make friends as I was overweight and wore raggedy clothes.

I eventually met a few girls who included me in their circle. One girl in particular took me under her wing.

"You ever tried weed before?" Christina asked me one day after school.

I shook my head, curious. I hated my home life and was struggling to fit in at school. Perhaps weed could provide the escape I needed from my not-so-wonderful life.

Suddenly, life was happening fast. I was making new friends, using drugs and meeting boys. I wondered what I'd been missing all this time. It felt good to be around people who wanted to be around me. At home, it seemed I was always in my mother's way. She was too absorbed with her own problems to pay much attention to me. Having a niche of my own was nice.

One evening, Christina suggested we go visit a guy she liked. When we arrived, he wasn't there, but his two roommates were. "You wanna get high?" one guy asked, pulling out a joint.

"Sure," I muttered. Getting high was part of my daily routine now. It didn't matter where I got pot or who I smoked it with, just as long as it took me away from my problems.

"We're gonna go get some food, okay? We'll be back." Christina hopped up and stumbled out the door with one of the guys.

This left just me and the other guy in the room, a guy I'd known for only an hour.

Suddenly, before I knew what was happening, the guy leaned toward me and began kissing me. "Guess it's just us now," he muttered, his smoky breath only inches from my face.

I winced and pulled back a bit, but he pressed in closer. The kissing continued, and then he slid off my pants. Inside, everything about me screamed, *No! This isn't right! Stop it!* But no words escaped my mouth. I was too high and confused to speak up. I succumbed to him, and we had sex on the couch. It was a painful, terrible experience, and when it was over, I felt used and dirty.

"I can't believe you had sex. That's so cool!" my friend gushed later when I told her what had happened. "You're not a virgin anymore, Bethany!"

"Yeah, cool," I muttered. I was anything but happy about the experience. I hadn't wanted to lose my virginity to a guy I barely knew while smoking pot on his couch. The entire situation sickened me. At that moment, I felt my identity had been robbed forever. If I had had sex that easily, perhaps I was a slut! Perhaps that's what I was meant to be all along. Maybe I was turning into my mother.

I threw myself into partying and sleeping with one guy after another. In a matter of months, I had become the girl I figured I was destined to be. To my surprise, my mother disapproved of my ways.

"I really don't want you running around with all those boys," she admonished me. "It's not healthy for a girl your age. You need to have some respect for yourself."

Respect? How can you lecture me like that? I thought to myself in disbelief. *You're the one who lets anyone into her bed!*

One evening, I came home to find my mother distraught. She had tried to cut her wrists with a butter knife and was sobbing hysterically. "He's going back to his wife," my mother cried in disbelief.

"Mom, I'm so sorry," I assured, running to her side.

"We were going to get married, but he went back to his wife. The nerve of him!" she sobbed.

I sighed and sat down beside her. "But he's married, Mom. He should be with his wife," I reminded her, though feeling her sadness as if it were my own.

"I know, I know …" Her voice trailed off as she looked up at me sadly. "I loved him, though."

My mother found another man shortly after, and they married. I dropped out of high school and moved into a party house with several friends.

Life was going nowhere fast, but I didn't much care. I spent my days drinking, doing drugs and meeting new guys. And for a while, this seemed like enough.

My oldest sister, Lisa, married and moved to Tigard, Oregon. She suggested I move there and give it a try. "It's really beautiful here, Bethany, and you already know people here." Lisa had always been the stable one with the good head on her shoulders.

Figuring I had nothing to lose, I followed Lisa to Oregon. I found work at a retail store but quit shortly afterward and continued partying. Meanwhile, my best friend, Christina, suggested I move to Philadelphia with her.

"You've gotta check it out. You'll love the big city," Christina insisted.

I moved to Philadelphia, hoping for a fresh start but hated it and moved back to Oregon within two months. The partying continued, and I floundered for the next several months, unsure of what to do next with my life.

Then one day, on a whim, I decided to move to Los Angeles. "I'm 20 years old and have my whole life ahead of me. I've gotta go see what's out there," I told my sister.

"Be careful, Bethany. L.A.'s a huge place. It can eat you alive if you're not careful," Lisa cautioned.

I didn't care. I was up for adventure. I packed my things and headed south. I worked for Cost Plus, an eclectic retail store, and was able to transfer to a store in L.A. I had no car at the time, but a friend who lived in the area gave me one to use when I arrived.

I soon discovered L.A., with its bright lights and buzzing nightlife, was not only exciting but expensive. As I began to price apartments to rent, I realized that rent alone could eat up my entire paycheck. I came up with a wonderful idea. If I lived in my car, I could save lots of money and be able to spend it on drugs instead of rent!

For a while, my plan seemed to work. I worked during the days, then spent the nights in my car or sleeping on the beach. I quickly made many friends who often let me crash on their couches. *Who needs a home, anyway?* I tried to convince myself.

One evening while working the night shift, I met a new co-worker. Al wasn't the most attractive guy I'd ever laid eyes on, but something about his charming personality captivated me.

"I did some time for drugs and just got out," Al confided in me one night. "I was involved in some gang stuff, too, but I'm tryin' to turn my life around for good now. Say, we should go out sometime."

"Uh, maybe," I replied casually. I was intrigued by Al but not sure I wanted to get involved with him.

Al was persistent, and I eventually agreed to go out with him. On our first date, I discovered he was 10 years older than me! I told myself this didn't matter nor did his past. He genuinely seemed to want to get his life back on track.

By our second date, I had slept with Al and was becoming increasingly attracted to him. Despite the fact that he'd done his share of partying in the past, Al seemed very against my current lifestyle.

"I want you to ditch those friends of yours," he told me shortly after we began dating. "They're no good for you.

You need to stick with me and stay sober."

At first, I thought this was a sweet gesture. Al was looking after me! I soon realized how controlling he was, however, and began to grow afraid. One month after we'd been dating, I was horrified to discover I was pregnant. How could I provide for a baby when I didn't even have a place of my own?

I managed to tell Al the news. "I'm pregnant," I croaked.

"It's cool. We'll get married. I'll take care of you guys," Al replied nonchalantly.

I felt trapped. I really didn't love Al and knew he wasn't the right one for me. Yet, what choice did I have? I certainly couldn't swing it on my own. I agreed to marry him, and we wed when I was four months pregnant.

Over the next couple of months, I began to see a new side of Al. While his concern for me had once seemed sweet, it now bordered on controlling. If I so much as looked at or spoke to another guy, Al objected.

"You're nothin' but a slut," Al sneered. He knew of my past and loved to rub it in my face.

I felt trapped, carrying his child. Maybe he was right. *I was nothing but a slut.* I thought about the days I'd sat in church with my mother, listening to the priest speak against fornication. "Fornicators are headed straight for hell!" the priest had boomed over and over. Perhaps God was punishing me for living so scandalously, and I was ruined forever!

One day as we rode the bus home after work, Al

leaned over to me and whispered, "I'm gonna beat your a** when we get home."

I gulped hard. I had grown terrified of Al since we married as I watched his once-sweet ways turn abusive. I hopped off the bus and started sprinting down the street. I knew I must have looked ridiculous, running at top speed with my five-month-pregnant belly jiggling up and down. I reached the house, ran inside and locked myself in the bathroom just before he arrived.

Al stormed inside and began beating on the bathroom door. "I'm sorry, baby. You know I was just messin' around. I would never hurt you. I love you, and I love our baby. I'm gonna take care of both of you, remember?" he cried out.

Yeah, right, I thought to myself. I'd heard this story before. Al would yell and curse or threaten me, and then seconds later, he'd be in my lap, trying to apologize. What was I going to do, though? Quit my job, run away and try to make it on my own? Who'd want a five-month-pregnant girl?

The emotional abuse continued with Al. "You're getting so fat," he sneered over and over. "Look how fat your a** is."

Tears burned my eyes at these remarks, but again, I felt helpless. Sometimes during our fights, I screamed back at him, but in the end, it did no good. Al had trapped me, and there was nowhere to go.

A few months before our son was born, Al lost his job. I suggested we move back to Oregon to be near my family.

Al agreed it was best, and we packed our things.

We moved in with my mother and stepfather for a few months. This allowed me to take maternity leave about a week before I delivered. Al treated them terribly, though. He complained about everything from the food they cooked to the fact that they smoked. "Your mom can't cook a decent meal to save her life," he muttered one night after dinner.

"I don't want to hear it," I snapped back. I was eight months pregnant and in no mood to hear Al complain. At least we had a roof over our heads and weren't living out of a car!

On July 16, after a very difficult labor and delivery, I gave birth to a beautiful little boy, whom we named Ray. One glance at Ray's sweet little face, and I was in love. I was also terrified. How could I mother a child under these conditions? I hated living with Al, yet I was tired of making poor choices. Maybe it was best to try to stick things out for Ray's sake. Besides, perhaps now that the baby had arrived, Al would change.

Since Al had no job, I was forced to return to my job at Cost Plus when Ray was only a few weeks old. I was weak and exhausted from the recovery and the sleepless nights but felt I had little choice. We needed to make money and get a place of our own.

When Ray was just 8 weeks old, I stepped out of the shower one morning to hear him screaming in the other room. I quickly grabbed a towel and rushed into the living room where Al was cuddling the baby.

"What happened?" I asked, still dripping wet. Ray was a fussy baby, but I had never heard him cry like that before.

"He's fine," Al assured me. "We were just playing airplane, and when I swooped him down, I dropped him. But don't worry. I caught him just before he hit the floor."

I sucked in my breath. "You dropped him?" I repeated angrily.

"Like I said, he's fine. I caught him. It just shook him up a little." He nuzzled his head in Ray's soft hair. "You're fine, aren't you, buddy?"

Still upset, I snatched Ray from his arms and pressed him to my chest. He looked okay, thankfully, but still … "Al, you've gotta be careful. He's just a tiny baby," I admonished, storming out of the room.

Later that night, Ray continued to fuss and refused to take his bottle. When I went to cuddle him, I heard a popping sound coming from his tiny shoulder. "Al, I think something's wrong with him. I think we should take him to the doctor," I called out.

"Nah, he's fine," Al kept insisting.

Still not convinced, I demanded Al drive us to the doctor. When we arrived, everything seemed to jump into fast forward. The doctors whisked the baby from us and began inspecting him. Suddenly, police arrived, along with social services.

"What's going on? Can someone tell me?" I asked, growing fearful.

Did they think we had harmed our baby?

No one seemed to be able to tell us what was happening. I ran from one doctor to the next trying to get answers. "Please, tell me what's going on," I pleaded. "Is Ray going to be all right?"

At last, one doctor sat me down and looked me squarely in the eye. "Your infant has a skull fracture and broken ribs. Do you realize how serious this is?"

"No, I had no idea …" I could scarcely breathe. "So what sort of care does Ray need to heal?" I asked, still not completely understanding.

"I don't think you get it," the doctor replied gravely. "Do you know how much force it takes to fracture a baby's skull? This is a very, very serious injury."

"Oh," I whispered, unable to speak. Tears filled my eyes as exhaustion overwhelmed me. Night had somehow turned into morning, and it was all I could do to keep my eyes open. Had I heard the doctor right? My son had been seriously injured?

The nightmare continued. A woman from social services approached Al and me in another room. "Your son will be taken into state custody until we can resolve this," she explained coldly. "You can stay here at the hospital to observe him while he is recovering, but you may not take him home."

I gasped. Ray would not be able to come home with us?! "That's absurd!" I cried. "We didn't do anything!" How could she possibly think we had harmed our son?

"You'll appear at juvenile court tomorrow morning for a hearing," she went on as though we were discussing dinner plans. "That will be all for now."

Sickened, I put my head in my lap and began to sob. How could this be happening? One minute we'd been at home, the next we were being told our son was going to be taken away from us!

"Tell me this isn't happening, Al," I moaned through my tears. "This is crazy, right?"

Al shook his head, his eyes glazed from fatigue. "Don't worry. I'm sure it's all a misunderstanding," he replied coolly.

We spent the night in a little hospital room with a giant window so we could be observed. I felt like a bug under a microscope, knowing officials were watching our every move. Did they truly not trust us?

After what seemed like the longest night of my life, we appeared in court the next morning. I was still in a state of shock as the woman from social services explained our case to the attorney. She then asked what we had to say for ourselves.

Al began rambling, giving the same story about how he'd been playing airplane with Ray and nearly dropped him. "I caught him, though. He's fine," he mumbled.

The attorneys didn't seem convinced. Ray was taken into state custody. Thankfully, they allowed him to go live with my sister temporarily. I was grateful for this but devastated at the same time. The moment we pulled out of the parking lot without my son, I felt as if my world had come crashing down on me.

The next few weeks were a flurry of investigations and

interrogations as the police and social services looked into our case. I was given a polygraph test, which I passed with flying colors. Next, I was given a psychiatric evaluation, which I also passed without any problems. *I can't believe I'm sitting here defending my parenting skills to these people*, I thought to myself as I answered question after question. Somewhere deep in the back of my mind, I began to wonder if I really was fit to be a parent after all.

After one of my counseling sessions, the social services worker arrived. "Can I be honest with you?" she asked, sitting down across from me. "You've checked out just fine, but it's your husband we're concerned about. You could probably have your son back tomorrow if your husband wasn't in the picture."

I was thrilled and terrified at the same time. I desperately wanted my son back home and would have done anything to be reunited with him. But how could I leave Al? Surely he would come after me. His anger had only escalated during this crisis. He had even threatened to kill my sister, saying he didn't want anyone touching our son. How could I take the risk of angering him further?

I continued working full-time, trying to take my mind off my nightmare. One night after work, I found a note in Al's jacket pocket. The note was from another girl and went into explicit detail about sexual things they had done together. My heart sank as I pored over the words. While a teeny part of me was relieved that this may be my "out," I was humiliated at the same time. How could he have betrayed me during my darkest hour?

I finally worked up the courage to leave Al and got permission from the state to stay at my sister's house until I could figure things out. "When I get back to the house, I want you out of here, understand?" I told Al firmly. My heart raced as the words escaped my mouth. I was finally standing up to this abusive man!

Al had failed the polygraph test, along with his other testing, and was found guilty of the charges pressed against him. He continued to fight and threaten me, but I refused to back down this time. For the sake of my future and my son's, I had to get out for good.

The next four years were a blur of custody battles as I fought for my son. I found an attorney who agreed to complete my divorce for me very inexpensively. Unfortunately, I didn't put much thought into the clause that read "Visitation will be as parties agree." Al's probation officer agreed that he could see Ray and me whenever he wanted, which terrified me to no end.

I returned to court where I pleaded with the judge to change the visitation status.

"Why is the visitation not in your divorce agreement?" the court demanded.

"I'm not sure," I replied, hanging my head. I wished I had gone over the divorce documents more thoroughly, but at the time, my main concern had been getting away from Al as quickly as possible.

Meanwhile, Al continued to threaten me like never before.

"I'm going to take Ray, and you'll never be able to find

him again," he snarled. He also threatened to bomb my car.

I was terrified for my life and for Ray's. So far, Al had not acted on any of his threats, but would he one day follow through? Each morning before work, I went out into the cold, started my car and let it run for several minutes before retrieving Ray from inside. I wanted to make sure Al hadn't really put a bomb inside my car.

At night, when I returned home from work, I locked all the doors and checked them over and over before heading to bed. I let Ray sleep with me, as I was too terrified of something happening to him while I slept. I began to feel like a prisoner inside my own life.

God, what have I done to deserve all this? I cried out one night. *Why is all of this happening to me?* I didn't talk to God very often. In fact, my only experience with God had been in my mother's Catholic church where God was portrayed as harsh and unloving. I had no idea what it meant to have a relationship with God or how badly I needed one to turn my life around.

Years of emotional confusion in my home and then in my relationship with Al had left my heart bruised and battered. I felt like a worthless nobody. I continued to throw myself into meaningless relationships, jumping from one guy to the next. I drank some as well, though I'd stopped smoking pot.

Ray was now 4 years old. One night as we ate dinner, he opened up to me. "Mommy, Daddy put my head in the toilet last week when I did somethin' bad. And the other night when I didn't want to eat my dinner, he pushed my face in a plate of food. It was hot and burned me real bad."

Anger welled inside of me. How could Al continue to get away with this? This was outright child abuse! Clearly, I had to get help.

I approached social services with my story. "There has to be something we can do," I pleaded. "You should hear the stories my son tells me. They're horrific."

"We could open a case for you, but until you have solid evidence of this abuse, I'm afraid there's nothing we can do," the caseworker replied matter-of-factly.

I was devastated. "So you mean to tell me I have to wait for something terrible to happen before you'll look into my case?" I asked incredulously.

The caseworker nodded. "I hate to put it that way, but I'm afraid the answer is yes."

I was outraged. My situation was a no-win game. If I didn't take Ray to visit his father, I'd be held in contempt of the court. And if I did take him, I could be risking his life at the hands of this abusive man. I was trapped!

I had moved away from Tigard to a suburb of Salem called Woodburn. I found an inexpensive preschool near my house and decided to enroll Ray. My sister had been watching him while I worked, which was a huge blessing, but I decided it was best for Ray to be around children his same age.

Ray enjoyed the preschool immensely. The school was part of a church, which I began attending. I knew I needed more in my life and had been contemplating going back to church for some time. I desperately wanted to get my act together again but didn't know how. I was still partying with my roommates on the weekends and sleeping around.

One morning, I stumbled out of bed in my rumpled clothes, reeking from last night's alcohol, and headed to the church. The moment I walked in the doors, I was amazed at how friendly everyone was. The pastor spoke about God as a loving being who desires a relationship with us. This was the first I'd heard about having a relationship with God. Wasn't he just some angry guy in the sky, ready to damn us to hell if we screwed up? I was curious to know more.

"We have a great young adults group here at the church," one girl told me. "You should check it out sometime."

"Thanks, I will," I replied sincerely.

The young adults group turned out to be more fun than I could have imagined. I had always assumed Christians were stuffy people who only sat around reading the Bible all the time. I was surprised to learn we'd be going on different outings and playing various sports.

"Good to see you, Bethany!" a guy called out as I showed up for a game one evening after work.

"You, too!" I returned, smiling and waving. I was thrilled to have found such a wonderful group to embrace me. They had been so kind and did not interrogate me with questions about my past as I'd feared they might do. I was amazed that these people who knew virtually nothing about me could accept me so easily.

One terrible night as I was in the middle of a volleyball game, Al showed up with Ray in his truck. When I opened the truck door, I grew sick. I knew Ray had been abused badly. I took him and ran into the church, where one of the preschool teachers met me inside.

"Oh, my gosh," she whispered as we sat down. "Are you okay?"

I was shaking terribly. "No, I'm not," I replied quietly, my heart racing as I replayed Al's stupid story over and over in my head. I turned to Ray. "Tell Mommy what happened, please," I begged him.

"I'm fine, Mom. I just want to go home," he insisted bravely.

I was to leave for Cincinnati the next morning for my best friend's wedding. I stopped by my sister's house to ask her advice.

"You can't put him on a plane unless you get him checked out, Bethany," my sister told me. "Look at him! It could be serious."

I took Ray to the hospital, where a very nice doctor checked him out. He was gentle and not at all invasive like the doctors in the past. "Can you tell me what happened, son?" he asked Ray gently.

At last, Ray opened up. With a quivering lip, he shared bits and pieces of his horrible story. "My dad got real mad at me, and he put his hands against my throat and lifted me against the wall. Then he pulled me up by my hair …"

I felt like I'd been punched in the stomach. How could

Al be capable of such terror? He was a monster!

The police arrived, along with some firemen, who Ray thought were very cool. I felt even sicker when they removed his shirt and found lacerations and bruises up and down his chest. "What now?" I whispered.

"Now, I think you have a case," the doctor replied.

Over the next few months, I worked hard to remove Al's parental rights. The court finally amended our divorce agreement, and Al was sent to jail. I could finally breathe a sigh of relief, knowing my son and I would be safe. I hoped to put this devastating ordeal behind us and move on.

I continued attending Hoodview Church in Woodburn. On August 21, 2005, I decided to get baptized. I wanted to profess to my church family that I loved God and wanted to live for him. I was still struggling with some of my ways from the past, but I was trying to make changes for the better. Each day was a fresh start, a new chance to live for Christ.

Little Ray always encouraged me to go to church. He loved going and learning about God. I had him dedicated at Hoodview Church, as well. It was a special moment for both of us.

In April 2007, Ray and I moved to Madras, Oregon, a little town of about 6,000 people, not far from Mount Hood. My current steady boyfriend lived there, and it seemed like a nice place to start over after all we'd been through.

As soon as the boxes were unpacked, I began my

search for a good church. My friend introduced me to Living Hope Christian Center, and I began attending occasionally. On my first visit, she insisted we sit in the front row, which made me rather uncomfortable. Unlike Hoodview Church with its large traditional choir, Living Hope boasted lively worship, complete with hand clapping and dancing. At first, I found this strange, but the worship eventually grew to be one of the things I loved most about the church.

After the worship ended, a youth group got up on stage and did a performance to a song about loving yourself. I was so moved that I started bawling right there in my seat.

"You okay?" my friend asked, nudging me.

I nodded and wiped my eyes. "Yeah, fine," I replied. I realized I had never done a very good job of loving myself. I just didn't know how. My home life had been unstable after my father walked out, and my mother had a difficult time showing love. The many men in my life had drifted in and out like the breeze, each one deepening my scars as they left. I realized for the first time how desperately I wanted to be loved and to love. But how was this possible with so much pain squeezing my heart?

Not wanting to go back into retail, I decided to open my own in-home daycare. I would be able to spend more time at home with Ray and would be working with children, which I loved.

I decided to make other positive changes in my life, this time for good. I stopped drinking altogether and told my boyfriend we could not sleep together anymore. I felt God was saying to me, "You are putting someone where I should be." I realized I had always used sex to cover the loneliness I felt inside. After praying about it, God revealed that he was leading my boyfriend and me in different directions, so we decided to break up, and for a while, I focused on things other than guys.

Money was tight in the daycare business. Often times, clients forgot to pay me, leaving me short when it came to paying bills. Eventually, my car was taken away when I could no longer afford to make the payments. I was devastated.

The morning after my car was repossessed, a couple I'd just met approached me. I had recently started watching their two little ones and hardly knew them at all. The woman handed me a set of car keys with a gentle smile. "We'd like you to have our car," she told me kindly.

I was speechless. People I hardly knew were giving me their car? "Thank you," I stammered, not sure how to accept such a gracious gift. "Are you — are you sure?"

She nodded. "Yes. We would be disobedient to God if we didn't give this to you."

The precious woman's name was Leigh. Out of this selfless act came a wonderful friendship. The car was nothing fancy, but the very idea that she had thought of me meant so much. I had never breathed a word about my financial difficulties to anyone! At that moment, I truly saw God working in my life, providing above and beyond what I could have asked for.

Leigh was a wonderfully genuine woman who had so much to offer. I had often thought about her statement regarding being "disobedient" to God. I asked her about it later, and she explained that God had put it on their hearts to give the car to me, and they simply wanted to obey him because they loved him and wanted to love others. I was blown away by her love for the Lord and wanted to emulate it.

During the next year, my faith grew like never before. The church in Woodburn had been a great launching pad for my spiritual life, but it was at Living Hope Christian Center that I truly began to seek out God and understand him for who he was. I was suddenly eager to live for God every day. I wanted nothing to do with the cares of the world that had encumbered me for so long. There was so much more freedom and joy in knowing Christ!

Leigh continued to mentor me, explaining things about God that had never made sense to me before. She prayed for me daily, which was a huge blessing. I had never had a friend who cared so much, not just for me but for my spiritual state, as well. "You'll never know how much that simple act meant to me," I told Leigh, referring to the car. "It was the kindest thing anyone had ever done for me." And I meant it. To me, Leigh was Jesus with skin on.

I continued to battle fear, something that had encumbered me since my days with Al. One day, God showed me a wonderful verse, Philippians 4:6: "Do not be anxious about anything, but in everything … present your requests to God." I read it over and over, thankful for such encouraging words. I did not need to be anxious as I slept at night or went about my day because my heavenly father was watching over me! I could trust in his perfect protection all the days of my life.

It seemed my life was going along swimmingly. My daycare business was thriving; I had many friends at my new church; my son was doing well; I was head over heels in love with the number one man in my life: Jesus! And then, in August 2008, came a devastating phone call that would change my life forever.

"Bethany," my sister whispered, "I want you to close your daycare down for the day. Then I want you to ask a friend to come over. Okay?"

Something was terribly wrong. "What happened, Lisa?" I interrupted, breathing fast.

"Mom — she fell — she's gone, Bethany." My sister could hardly get the last words out.

Dead? Mom's dead? Surely I had heard her wrong. My mother dead? It couldn't be true! I had just talked to her a few days ago!

Unable to speak, I stared at the phone, refusing to believe that my own mother had been taken away from us. My heart raced as I tried to speak. "Are you sure, Lisa?" I cried out at last.

"Yes."

I learned over the next few hours that my mother, who had been addicted to painkillers for most of her adult life, had been sleepwalking and slipped and fell. She broke her neck, which killed her instantly. It was a terrible freak accident that left our entire family reeling.

The few days following my mom's death were a blur. I wandered around in a fog, wavering between denial and anger. My faith, which had grown so strong, felt almost nonexistent for a few moments. How could God have taken my mother from me? Yes, she hadn't been perfect, but she was still my mother! Ray had grown to love her over the past few years since he'd started spending time with her. How could I explain to my son that his grandma was gone?

My church friends came over to support me as we prepared for the funeral. I was so grateful for their love and concern but was grieving so badly, I could hardly function. On the way to the funeral home, my little car died in the 108-degree heat. Tears streamed down my cheeks as I tried over and over to restart the engine. *God, where are you in this? I don't feel you!*

I called my pastor, hoping he might have a few encouraging words for me. "I feel terrible not knowing if my mom's in heaven with the Lord or not," I cried through my tears. "I just want to have peace about this."

My pastor was so kind and ministered to me during my darkest hour. "God has his reasons and timing for everything, Bethany," he assured me. "He is the greatest comfort one can know. It may not feel like he's with you right now, but he is. The moment you asked him into your life, he promised never to leave or forsake you."

I took great comfort from his words. Once again, I

wondered what I would have done without my precious church family.

"Bethany, I think you should know that before your mother died, she was praying the Rosary and reading her Bible a lot," my stepfather told me one day.

"Really?" I replied, hopeful. My mother may not have been a strong Catholic when she died, but I prayed that perhaps God saw her heart and that she truly had turned her life over to him before she passed away.

Shortly after, I began working with the youth at church, which I enjoyed immensely. I saw myself as a teen in many of their faces: a lonely girl, trying to fit in, hurting inside, just wanting to be loved. Getting to know teens isn't easy, but I am attempting to give them what I always needed: someone who thought I was worth the effort.

***

"Well, Bethany, it's unanimous. We want you to have the job," my pastor told me over the phone, his voice bubbling with enthusiasm.

"Really?" I squeaked, hardly able to believe the good news. I had interviewed for a position as the church secretary at Living Hope Christian Center a few hours before. I had been rather intimidated, as several other very qualified women from the church also applied. I was considering quitting my daycare business and felt God strongly urging me to apply for the job. On a whim, I turned in my resume and was delighted when they chose to interview me. Never in a million years did I dream I had a shot at actually getting the job, though!

"I'm honored. I don't know what to say," I replied after a long pause. "Thank you!"

As I hung up the phone, I almost felt like twirling cartwheels across the room. *God, you are so good,* I prayed. *Your grace is something I'll never quite comprehend. You had your hand on my life, even when I could not see it, even when I did not acknowledge you were there. You waited patiently for me to come to you, drawing me to you through people who love you the way I want to love you. I don't deserve this life, but I thank you all the same. Thank you for taking this once messed-up girl and giving her a second chance.*

"Hey, Mom, I'm done!" Ray called out from the other room, holding a picture he'd been hard at work on. Ray was wonderfully artistic, a quality I hoped to bring out in him more as he got older.

"Great job, bud!" I praised him. I watched him scamper off, his tousled hair bringing a smile to my face. I prayed one day God would bring that special man into our lives who could be the father and husband we needed. In the meantime, though, we had a father who loved us unconditionally, a father who would never leave our sides: Jesus Christ! And in his arms, we were truly safe.

YOU WILL BE SCORCHED
THE STORY OF MARIE
WRITTEN BY MIKE NAGEL

"I don't know if I love you anymore."

Greg's words came slowly as he measured them out. Each one hit me like a punch — *I Don't Love You* — and I couldn't believe he was serious. But he was. His face was drawn and gray, as solid as stone.

"What — what do you mean?" I asked, stunned.

"I don't know, Marie," he said, looking away. "I still feel the same I always have about you. But I don't think it's love."

We'd been married for five years. Five years! We had two children — a boy and a girl. At the time, we both went to school full-time and worked part-time jobs. There were plenty of stresses in our lives as we struggled to make ends meet and raise our kids, but I didn't think it was anything more than plenty of other couples dealt with. From the outside, we looked like a happy churchgoing family.

"What is it then?"

"I don't know. Maybe it's love. But maybe it isn't."

I looked at him briefly, meeting his eyes, then looked away at the floor, withdrawing.

Is it my fault? I thought. *Maybe I'm not good enough.*

***

STRENGTH FOR TODAY

"Just look at her hair, Marie," Grandma said. "Isn't it just the most beautiful thing you've ever seen?"

My sister's hair was dark. She got that from Grandma, who was one-quarter American Indian. My hair was fair and blond. While she didn't say it out loud, Grandma's point was clear — I wasn't as pretty as my sister.

"Yeah, sure," I mumbled, but Grandma didn't bother to listen to my response. She wasn't looking for an answer to her question; she didn't need one. It was rhetorical, stated for the purpose of praising my sister, just as much as for putting me down. For every praise my sister got, I heard another reminder that I wasn't as good as her.

Another time, Grandma watched the two of us walk up the stairs. We were at a hotel with an exposed staircase. I was 12 years old. My sister was 16 months older than I. She'd already hit her growth spurt and gained about six inches in height on me.

"Look at you two girls," said Grandma. "Your legs are just the same width."

I got the message. It was obvious. My legs were chunky and not long and slender like my sister's.

If she spilled the milk, it was an accident. If I did it, it was because I was too young to be careful or too clumsy or too stupid. My good grades in school were just a matter of luck. And Grandma never once told me that I was beautiful.

I tried to not let it bother me, but it did. The more I fought to push those words out of my head, the louder they screamed. *She is beautiful. You are not! She's thin.*

YOU WILL BE SCORCHED

You are fat! As desperate as I was to ignore the criticism, I was just as desperate to prove it wrong. So I threw myself into being the best at everything I did. I started playing sports year round — volleyball, basketball, track and tennis. I worked hard to be the best, challenging myself to run faster, jump higher and be stronger in the hopes of winning approval.

Boys scared me then. They were loud and intimidating, always shoving each other and horsing around. I couldn't handle that. Plus, anytime I showed interest in one, he always seemed to find reasons to avoid me. I'd asked three boys in high school to Sadie Hawkins dances, and two of them said no. Their excuses sounded good enough, at first — too much homework, family vacation or whatever — but the more I thought about it, the less sure I was they were telling me the truth.

Maybe I'm just not good enough.

***

It wasn't a surprise when, after I'd graduated high school (with a 3.7 GPA and an "outstanding senior girl" award, by the way), I fell for the first guy in college who seemed to like me. He was attracted to me and didn't think of reasons to not see me. In fact, he went out of his way to spend time with me. He made me feel wanted. He made me feel loved.

A year after we met, Greg and I got married. Five years later, he told me he didn't know if he ever loved me. With those words, all of the pain, doubt and confusion I'd felt growing up came rushing back.

After this revelation, we decided to stick together. We had Sarah and Josh to think of. And I never believed in divorce. I was convinced that I'd married this man for life, for better or for worse, and we could work through whatever came up.

Greg had a habit of making frequent confessions to me. He thought that admitting what was going on — questioning his love, for example — was helpful in working through our problems. Maybe it was for him, but I came to dread the confessional sessions. He'd tell me about asking a co-worker out to dinner while I was out of town, passing it off as just something between friends while at the same time revealing she'd turned him down because "she didn't date married men." He told me the whole story matter-of-factly, then considered it "case closed" and moved on, leaving me behind in a wake of unanswered questions and confusion.

Whenever he felt attracted to someone else, his guilt drove him to tell me about it and ask my forgiveness. But I wasn't strong enough to hear about it. The first time it happened, I was eight months pregnant. My back ached from the baby weight I'd put on. It was hard enough to get out of bed and face the bathroom mirror every day, thinking that I'd never be the skinny girl I was in high school ever again, without having my husband telling me he was strongly attracted to someone else. To top it off, she was a friend of mine, a good one, and far thinner and more beautiful than I thought I could be — pregnant or not.

I can't blame him entirely. I don't think he consciously tried to break down my self-esteem, but that's what he did. Greg's mother had been thin in her younger years but then struggled with weight later in life, and he didn't want the same thing to happen to me.

"Hold your stomach in to make it look thinner," he told me.

Anytime I complained that what he said was hurtful, he turned it around, telling me that he said these things to help me. But they had the opposite effect — they only hurt.

When the pamphlets from a nearby plastic surgery clinic showed up in our mailbox, I asked him what it was all about.

"What is this?" I asked, holding up the shiny pamphlet.

"It's just from the clinic! I thought you might want to look at these," he stammered. "I thought you might want a nose job or a breast enlargement to make yourself feel better."

Each month, I threw another postcard mailing from the clinic into the trash. The junk mail screamed at me from the can, "Lose weight fast! Get the body of your dreams!"

That's it — I'm just not good enough.

***

STRENGTH FOR TODAY

Fifteen years in and we'd been married for almost half our lives. The kids were growing up. Sarah was 14 and getting ready for high school. Josh was 12 and just becoming a man himself. Greg and I had made it through the rocky stretches, including a nine-month separation two years prior, but I thought it would work out. Sure, we fought at times. Money was always tight, and stress levels always shot up at the end of the month, but somehow we always managed to have enough. And we had the usual miscommunication problems most couples face. He'd want to stay up hours each night talking, but I couldn't keep my eyes open, knowing I'd have to work the next day. But I thought we'd worked out the major problems. *We can do this marriage thing*, I thought.

***

"I think I've found the love of my life," he told me. "It's real. I want a divorce."

I was stunned. Once again, I'd opened up to be shut down. I wasn't even sure how long they'd been having an affair, but I found out it had been going on for months. Suddenly, our marriage was over. But he didn't move in with his new girlfriend right away. Rather, our daughter moved into our room, and he took her room over. I would lie awake at night and listen to his footsteps as he came home late. It wasn't hard for me to imagine exactly where he'd been. Finally, he left us for good.

At the age of 34, I found myself alone. My husband

had left me for another woman, and I hadn't been good enough for him. I'd lost him to someone else. Now it was up to me to care for the kids. I did my best to manage. For a year, I lived in a fog. I went to work like a robot, stiffly going through the motions of daily tasks before going home and crying myself to sleep many nights. I couldn't face my own depression, staying busy and focusing outward rather than inward. I lost my appetite and dropped 20 pounds in 12 months.

Later in life when we were looking back on things, Sarah told me that it was like I'd died emotionally. Physically, I was there, but otherwise, I was completely detached.

Our broken little family kept on going to church, week in and week out, seeking comfort there. We'd always gone, and it seemed like we needed it more now than ever before. I sang and played keyboard every Sunday morning, and I threw myself into the music ministry with renewed vigor. If I could just get something right — maybe it was the worship team — then I'd be okay.

The first time I saw Jeff, I was playing keyboard onstage. I looked out over the congregation, people standing and singing, and I saw him toward the back. From my position up front, I knew most of the regular churchgoers — if only by face rather than name.

Oh, he's handsome, I thought.

Focus on your music, came the reply from the logical side of my brain. *Guys are the enemy, right?*

I kept on playing, focusing on the sheet music and

chords but found my eyes drifting toward the back. *On second thought, it's hard to tell what he looks like — FOCUS!*

He kept his head down throughout most of the service, so it was hard to get a glimpse of his face. But I felt drawn to him nonetheless.

This game of visual cat-and-mouse, one side of me trying to sneak glances and the other side offering swift, strict correction, continued for about six months. It was never anything more than that. He didn't meet my furtive looks, and I never worked up the courage to talk to him.

A friend of mine changed that. She wasn't married and led our church's singles class.

"Marie, why don't you come check out the singles class?" she asked.

"No way, that's not for me. I don't want to meet any new guys. I'm done with all that."

"It's not about meeting people," she replied, feigning hurt. "It's just a great class with some fun friends."

"So why do you want me to come?"

"You'd love it!" she said. "We've had a few new regulars sign up, and they're all guys. I'm feeling a little outnumbered. You should come."

"Oh, fine," I relented. "I'll keep you company."

"Besides," she added, "there's this one guy — he's really sweet. He's too young for me, but I think you'd like him."

"Not a chance!"

I went to the singles group, anyway, guard up and fully

prepared to find something wrong with every guy in the room. In fact, I prided myself on finding a chink in every guy's armor within five minutes of meeting him. I was done with men. I gave marriage a go, and all it gave me in return was heartbreak. There was a problem with my plan, though. After I met Jeff, I couldn't find a chink in his armor. Each week, I'd go expecting him to make an off-hand comment or admit to some defect that would prove to be his undoing. But each week, I left disappointed. There didn't seem to be anything wrong with him. *He was*, I grudgingly admitted to myself, *a really nice guy. In fact, he just might be — perfect?*

No, I couldn't think like that. I wasn't ready.

But when he smiled, I knew I was in trouble. He seemed fun loving and comfortable, totally sure of himself. It was his confidence, the way he eased into every conversation that won me over. That and the way he carried himself, so smooth and sure. Before long, and despite my best efforts, I was intrigued.

The holidays were coming, and work put together a Christmas party. The year before, I'd gone with my husband, joining the other happy couples in welcoming the holidays. This year, I didn't have a date — the divorce was final, and my happy marriage had ended in tragedy. I was going to be the wallflower, a dateless loser.

But what about Jeff, I thought. *Couldn't I invite him? We'd just go as friends — it wouldn't mean anything.*

We'd gotten to know each other pretty well, just joking around and mingling during the weeks prior, but I still felt nervous asking him and put it off until the last minute. One week before the party, I finally got up the nerve to call and invite him, fully expecting him to say no.

"Just for fun!" I added, laughing lightly. "No pressure if you can't make it."

"Sure, I love parties! I'd be glad to come."

The night of the party, he showed up with a bouquet of flowers for me and a pound of chocolate for the kids. No one had ever shown up with either for any date — including my ex-husband — and now some knight in shining armor showed up with both!

Sarah was instantly won over by the chocolates and immediately set about digging through the box for her favorites. Josh, though, was not so easily taken.

"Mom," he said, tugging on my sleeve and pulling me aside while Jeff chatted with Sarah, "I don't think you should be dating anyone."

"Don't worry; I'm not," I explained. "But I can't back out now; he's standing right here!"

"I don't like it."

"Well, I can't back out now. We've got to be at dinner in half an hour!"

Jeff came over just then and started talking to Josh about the things he was into, sliding just as easily into conversation with my son as he did at the singles meetings. As the two guys chatted man-to-man about Legos and video games, I had to smile — Jeff was winning him over pretty quickly. We spent a wonderful evening together at the party, and Jeff was the perfect gentleman the entire time, even offering his arm to make sure I didn't slip on the icy ground.

The next day was a Sunday, and Jeff came up to us after church.

"Hey, guys!" He smiled, inquiring, "How about I take you out to brunch today?"

I opened my mouth to reply when I realized he wasn't talking to me. He was looking at my son, Josh.

"Sure!" came the reply, without an ounce of hesitation.

"Heck, Mom, free food!" he told me later when I asked him why he agreed.

***

We began dating. We hadn't been seeing each other very long — just a couple weeks — when Jeff told me he needed to talk. I took a breath and prepared myself.

Here it comes. You're not good enough, and he's going to leave now that both you and the kids are attached.

It wasn't that, though. Jeff wasn't planning on breaking things off. He just felt that it was the right time to tell me about his past.

He didn't remember much about his childhood. When he said that, I chalked it up to a bad capacity for memory. I didn't find out it went much deeper than that until later.

He nodded and shrugged. He also told me why he'd started going to our church.

"You know, I'd been working as a counselor at this conference center."

He'd told me about the job before. It was at a youth camp, which was packed during the summers. It's where he'd discovered he got along well with kids, especially the boys, who all looked up to him.

"I — you see …" He looked embarrassed. "I was forced to resign that job. Parents were complaining."

"What were they complaining about?"

"Well, I was having conversations with the younger counselors and some of the kids. We'd talk about personal stuff, and I think the parents felt it was inappropriate. So I had to quit. It's my fault, really — I let things go too far."

"Well, is it a problem now?"

"No. I'm doing some counseling with the pastor at church. He's the one who asked me to talk to you. We thought you should know."

"Okay."

Honestly, I didn't think much of the conversation. What struck me the most wasn't what he told me but how uncomfortable he was doing it. But I was impressed with his willingness to talk about it before our relationship went any further. He'd tell me later that he never opened up like that to anyone, especially a woman. None of his relationships lasted more than two or three dates. Fear of commitment or having to let someone else in drove him away.

***

Three months later, Jeff took me on a romantic date.

YOU WILL BE SCORCHED

He booked us a table for two on a dinner train that also featured a live mystery theater performance during the course of the evening. When we walked into the train car, I found a bouquet of flowers in a vase on our table. It was the only one that had any flowers, which I thought was odd.

During the performance, a cast member pointed out the window, shouting something about a bridge. I turned to peer into the dark to have a look but couldn't see anything. When I turned back to the table, Jeff was on one knee beside me. He took my hand in his and showed me an engagement ring.

"Marie, you would make me the happiest man in the world if you would consent to be my wife."

My mouth dropped open in surprise. I was taken completely aback. The play had paused as the cast, who were all in on the proposal, along with the entire dining car, stopped to watch. *We* were the ones on stage now. All I could do was stare at him.

"Will you marry me?" he repeated.

"Yes!"

I would've probably liked more time to think, but what else can you say when everyone's watching?

***

The first couple years of marriage were great. Jeff was fun and easy to get along with. He never talked about other women and always treated me like a lady — a happy departure from my previous marriage. He even made me feel thin and beautiful, telling me that I was too skinny in old pictures. He was great with the kids, too. We ate meals together, went to church together and even took a fabulous vacation to Disneyland. Life with Jeff was all about fun, fun, fun!

Every now and then, though, I started to see small dark spots in the brightness that was life with Jeff. Like the sun disappearing behind a cloud on a bright day, his face would darken, and his words grew sharp. But then the happiness came back quickly. The moments were fleeting and far between. At least they were at first. Together, we built our dream house and settled into life as a family. It felt like things were perfect again.

After two years, though, I started noticing a change. Jeff's dark moods seemed to come with more frequency, and they lasted longer than before. The happy times seemed to grow more distant until he was in a funk more often than not. He stopped smiling as much, and everything seemed to bother him, like his nerves were constantly on edge.

"I can't eat this. I don't like it," he'd snap at the dinner table.

"But, Jeff, you haven't even tried it."

"I don't want to, Marie," he replied, his voice cutting. "You know I can't eat nuts and seeds. I hate the way they feel, always getting caught in your teeth."

"Just try it, please."

"No! I'm not eating it."

YOU WILL BE SCORCHED

It was a childish way to act, one that our family wasn't used to. The kids had been taught to try everything on their plates. It was strange for them to see a grown man throwing temper tantrums.

I started giving him space, hoping that these moods would pass. When we were in public, visiting with church friends or running errands, he was fine. But when we were at home or alone, he grew dark and reserved. The more space I gave him, the more he withdrew.

I thought his job might be stressing him out. He worked long hours on the swing shift, so most nights he didn't get home until 1:30 in the morning. He'd come home, tired after a day's work, and spend an hour or two unwinding by himself before coming to bed. I didn't know what he did during that time, but I figured he just needed to de-stress.

***

"Mom, I need to talk to you."

"What is it, Josh?" I asked.

My son led me to the computer.

"I've gotta show you this. I think Jeff might be gay. Look what I found."

He moved the mouse to a window in the toolbar and popped up a series of pornographic sites. I saw pictures of naked men; some appeared to be very young. I trawled through about 10 pornographic images, with not a single female to be seen.

"That's enough," I told my son. "Turn it off."

I didn't want my child to keep looking, and I didn't need to see any more.

I waited for Jeff to come home from work. The hours passed, and with each tick of the clock's hands, another unanswered question popped into my head.

When he finally got home after midnight, my mind was buzzing.

"I need to talk to you."

"Okay." He looked simultaneously surprised I was awake and nervously guilty, like he knew he'd been caught.

"Are you unhappy in this marriage?"

"No, of course not!"

"Well, then," I exhaled, "is there anything you need to tell me?"

"Um." He looked away, skittishly. "No, I don't think so."

"Do you want a divorce?" My voice shook with anger.

"No! Why would you even ask that?"

I swore. "What do you think you're trying to do?"

I pointed to the computer and told him what my son had found, what I'd seen, what I knew he was doing every single night after work instead of coming to bed with his wife.

Jeff's face paled. His lips moved, but nothing came out except a weak gasp. He tried again, clearing his throat. His mouth formed words, but nothing came out, so he gave up and stared at the floor.

"Are you gay? Are you confused or something?" I asked him quietly.

"N-n-no," he stammered, "I don't think so. I mean, I don't want to be!"

"I've already been left by a man for another woman," I told him. "I don't think I can take being left for a man!"

"I wouldn't do that! I married you, and that's what I want. I'm not gay!"

We ended up talking for hours, Jeff continually reassuring me that he was in this marriage for good and there wasn't anything wrong with me. He said he was just insecure. That's why he had to look at other men to reassure himself that he was normal. He sounded like a woman, insecure about the size of her breasts. The more I listened, the more I believed this was something we could work through. I didn't believe in divorce, and we'd been so happy — surely this was just a little bump in the road. No couple is perfect. *I've finally found the chink in his armor*, I thought to myself.

***

Several months later, I was driving home from work when I started composing a song in my head. I was still heavily involved with the worship team at church and had even recorded a CD of my own. Music had always been a refuge for me, a place I could go when I was troubled or needed comfort.

As I drove, I prayed. Snatches of words and melody

appeared in my head, and the message was powerful.

Press on.

Never give up the fight.

I knew this song, once finished, was going to be a great encouragement to someone in need.

Little did I know that someone was me.

I arrived home and went about my usual business in the house, putting things away, straightening up and humming snatches of the new song.

Press on.

Never give up the fight.

The telephone rang, and I picked it up. It was Jeff's boss.

"Hi, Marie," he said. "Do you know where Jeff is?"

"He's at work, right?"

"No, he's not. He never showed up. You probably want to call the county jail."

Before I could call, the phone rang again. It was Jeff.

"Where are you?"

"I'm in jail."

"What?!"

"They asked me to come down to the police station for questioning. They asked me if I'd touched this boy. I told them I did."

A few months earlier, two boys from church had spent the night. The older one accused Jeff of fondling him while he was sleeping. Jeff said it was true; he had touched the boy, but it was an accident. He'd been going downstairs to get a glass of milk. On his way down, he went into the bedroom where the boys were sleeping, bent down to tickle the boy and say goodnight. Jeff claimed his hand slipped, and he missed. He was embarrassed, and, when the boy didn't wake up or say anything, he just left the room.

He made it sound so plausible, so I believed him. It had to be an accident. He was my husband, and I'd stand by him, no matter what. This must all be an embarrassing mistake. The judge arraigned him and released him the next day. Since there were children in our house, the judge didn't feel it was right to send Jeff home to us, so Jeff went to live with his mother and stepfather.

Three days before Christmas, Jeff and his parents were visiting our house. The police knocked on our door and took him away. Another victim had come forward.

The court held the arraignment the next day, and the courtroom was filled — both by the news media and with our friends and fellow church members. Jeff and I appreciated the support of the latter. It was difficult to hold my head up when I knew I'd have to watch my husband sitting slumped before the judge.

I ran into a friend in the courtroom, and she beckoned me over. Her lips were pursed.

"I need to tell you something," she said, grabbing my elbow and pulling me away from the crowd.

"I asked my son if Jeff ever touched him." She paused to collect herself. "He told me yes — Jeff fondled him. He must have thought he was asleep, but he wasn't. He was awake the whole time!"

I didn't know what to think. I was shocked and appalled. It was the exact same scenario. It couldn't have been an accident after all. I'd believed what Jeff told me — it was an accident; he was insecure — and now I glimpsed the entire, awful truth.

I confronted him before the hearing.

"Is this true?" I demanded after repeating the story.

His face fell. He looked like he'd been punched.

"Yes," he mumbled. "I won't blame you a bit if you walk out of here and leave me."

I spent the rest of the afternoon in a daze, not believing this was happening to me.

The judge released Jeff again to his stepfather's care so he didn't have to spend Christmas in jail. He may as well have, though, because all of the usual joy and celebration had been completely sucked out of the house. In its stead was a hulking blackness that no one acknowledged as we sat around the table with forced smiles plastered on our numb faces.

After Christmas, Jeff and I sat down to talk in his stepfather's trailer. There were three more victims. This time, they were younger boys, and I'd had all I could take. I was ready to divorce him.

"I knew this would happen!" Jeff was upset, visibly agitated. "I knew people would start lying. I didn't do anything to those kids."

As I listened to him, I realized he was telling the truth about the new accusations. Thoughts of divorce slipped away.

YOU WILL BE SCORCHED

We could still get through this. But I had to know everything.

"You're my husband, and I'll stand by you," I told him. "But I cannot keep doing this if I have to find everything out from other people. If one more bomb goes off in my face, I'm leaving."

Jeff took the ultimatum well. He explained that he did these things — looking at pornography, sending inappropriate emails and touching boys — because he was insecure. He was worried whether or not he was normal, whether he was big enough and if the boys had the same anxieties. It was a warped way of thinking, and he knew it. During the dark times, when his smile and happiness disappeared, he struggled with his past pushing him into a downward spiral of perversion. He told me everything, in detail, about how he touched the boys. He vehemently denied some of their accusations (three younger boys had come forward with exaggerated claims) but admitted to the others.

He'd told me before that he didn't remember much about his childhood. I found out the reason for the memory lapse went much deeper than mere forgetfulness.

"No, literally, I can't remember anything until I was 12 years old. Before that, it's just snippets, like snapshots taken out of context."

"What do you mean?"

"Well," he hesitated, "I remember seeing my uncle naked. But I don't know why. I just know it made me feel funny. I must have been really young then.

"There is this one thing I remember from when I was 8," he continued. "I was in my grandparents' kitchen. My uncle was in the other room, and I was alone. They had a chopping block on the counter, full of heavy steel knives. I can remember staring at the handles, wishing I could reach out, draw a blade and stab my uncle in the chest."

"Why?"

"I don't know. I can't remember."

"That's terrible."

He nodded and shrugged. I realized that he'd repressed much of his childhood for a reason — something horrible had happened to him.

As I listened to him, I was strangely glad that we were digging deep into the root of the problem. I knew he needed help, but I never believed him to be dangerous. However, I could see that he teetered on the edge of something far worse. He was living life on the edge of the knife, and I still hoped that I could help steer him in the right direction.

The district attorney originally asked the judge for a 25-year sentence. But we had plea bargained down to a two-year prison sentence, with 10 years of probation, as long as Jeff pled guilty on two counts. Our expensive lawyer and the fact that our friends and I continued to show support didn't hurt, either.

***

Josh's 16th birthday was the same day as Jeff's transfer to prisoner processing. My son and I had decided to have a quiet pizza party for two at our house as part of a muted celebration. We'd picked up the food and were on our way home when we saw smoke in the distance. As we neared our neighborhood, the air became black, heavy with soot, and we saw flames in the fields beyond. It was a brushfire started by accident, and the winds were pushing it toward our development.

There were fire trucks everywhere throughout the neighborhood. Everywhere, that is, but where my house was. I didn't see the one pulling up behind me. As we pulled into the driveway, the smell of smoke was overpowering. Flames had rushed through the field behind our house and were licking at the base of the wooden backyard fence.

I ran inside to grab our dog, embers from the burning brush falling through the air around me as the winds whipped the flames into a frenzy. I snatched up our dog, looked around for anything else to save, thought better of it and ran for the front door.

By that point, the firemen were ordering us back, and there was nothing we could do but drive a couple blocks away and watch. As the sun set, we saw the familiar shapes of the neighborhood — rooftops, cars and the façade of our own home — backlit in an eerie silhouette of flame as the trees on the back of our property burned. It was like watching everything you believe in, everything that kept you safe, burn to the ground.

"You know," I told Josh, "our house probably won't be

here in the morning."

"Yeah, I know, Mom."

"But we'll be okay," I said, putting my arm around his shoulder. "We can always build another one."

"Yeah."

But as it turned out, the wind died down and changed direction. The firefighters took on the seemingly out-of-control blaze and put it out. The flames had crept to our fence, but that's as far as they went — our place had been spared, but everything around it was burned black. The smell of charred debris was overwhelming.

I went out the next morning to survey the damage. On both sides of the house, our property line was black, as if some giant had bent down and colored in the other lots with a permanent marker. The polyester mesh trampoline had melted from the heat, shrinking down to a ball in the middle of the backyard. All of the surrounding trees were dead.

I went to the back fence and looked at the line of scorched earth and the blackened boards. Then I heard a voice speak quietly and clearly.

"It's going to get hot, Marie. You will get scorched, but you won't be consumed."

It was God sending comfort my way. And I knew he wasn't talking about the house.

***

With Jeff in prison, money was tight. I worked five

jobs to make sure we had food on the table and the mortgage was paid every month. I'd already made it through nine months without his income.

I ran a medical supply company out of my garage as one of the five jobs. One day, I had to clean a hospital bed that an outpatient had used in their home for years. I'm pretty sure the sponge I took to it was the only one it had seen in all that time. Rotten food, rust and fecal matter clung to the sides. *And the smell* — it made me gag just to be in the same room, which was unusual for me. In all my years as a nurse, I'd never seen something so disgusting.

By this time, I had also begun volunteering at a local boys' prison, leading small Bible studies and helping out with the music during their services. I'd seen the need for people to reach out to prisoners through my own husband's time in jail.

While I cleaned, I prayed for the boys — most of whom were around 16 years old. Many had been sexually abused, their histories causing them to lash out in violence, and the prison was full of sex offenders.

I heard a voice whisper to me just as it had the day after the fire.

"Will you clean toilets for me?"

"What?"

"Will you clean toilets for me?" the voice repeated.

Then it hit me. Who are those people in society that we just want to lock up and throw away the key? Who do we recoil from in fear and distaste? They're the sex offenders. God was asking me to love them because he loved them the same as he does every human being.

Yes, Lord, I will clean toilets for you!

"Jeff is your first assignment."

***

Jeff spent his time in prison. I tried to visit as often as I could, but he was five hours away, and the costs were prohibitive. With only one income to cover the mortgage, I had to work as much as I could. But we did write letters to each other, and hardly a day went by that I didn't hear from him.

He seemed to be doing well. "I'm learning from my mistakes," he wrote. As he bore his soul to me, telling me about his challenges and victories, I felt like we were communicating on a deeper level than we ever had before. "I'm sorry, Marie. I'll make it all up to you. I will be a new man — the man God wants me to be."

We made it through the two-year sentence and set to work repairing our marriage. He was happy again after he was out, and it was good to have him home. I monitored his computer usage, and he wasn't allowed to come in contact with minors (Josh, at this time, was living with his dad, and Sarah had graduated high school). Jeff gladly attended all of the state-mandated classes, as well as men's groups and counseling sessions at our church. He even wrote updates for our pastor a couple times a year to keep him up to speed on his progress.

For eight years, we worked at building up trust and

learning how to be a loving couple. Jeff apologized in front of the entire congregation at our church and found, probably to his surprise, more forgiveness and help than rejection. He didn't show any signs of stumbling back to his old ways and instead displayed a constant desire to work to be a better man.

That was until late in 2007 when I noticed Jeff starting to retreat within himself, just like he used to a decade earlier. He became moody, brows knitted and face dark. Our communication began to break down again, but I hoped it was just a phase. I alerted him that we needed to talk.

"What's going on?" I asked him a couple weeks later.

"You know, I don't know …" His voice trailed off, and he looked away.

"What's going on?" I repeated.

"I guess I'm still struggling with the whole thing. I think … I think I might be gay."

"You've got to be kidding me."

"I might be."

"After 12 years and everything we've gone through, I don't think I'm the answer." I threw up my hands. "I think we're going to have to separate until you get things straightened out."

Six months later, a friend of mine found Jeff's profile on MySpace. He'd listed his status as "Single" and "Gay." I had hoped he'd be able to work through things, but it looked like he'd made his choice. I submitted the divorce papers, which the judge signed immediately. It was April Fool's Day.

***

While others may come and go in my life, God will never leave me nor forsake me — through the rejection, two divorces, a criminal trial and everything in between. I know that I am never far from his love and protection. I live to worship him and bring him joy. The greatest happiness I feel is when I know that I brought a smile to God's face. It's why I can keep going, day in and day out.

I've made Proverbs 3:5-6 my life's motto: "Trust in the Lord with all your heart and lean not on your own understanding; in all your ways acknowledge him, and he will make your paths straight." Where those paths end, I don't know. But I fully believe that my story isn't over. Only half of it's been written.

***

I remember my first time going into a prison *alone*. For a woman, walking into the foreboding concrete-and-barbed-wire structure where murderers, rapists and drug dealers are kept is terrifying.

I'd been to several different prisons with a group called the Freedom Team before. This time, though, I was again on my own. I'd run into the chaplain of this particular facility, told him how I felt called to do prison ministry — I now tell the inmates I'm a prison ministry junkie who works as a nurse to support her habit — and he invited me to come share my music. But the weekend I went, the chaplain was double-booked, and a different chaplain and his wife were there to greet me.

There were four chapel services that weekend. The first three went well, but then there was a stabbing in Complex 3 just before I was to go in for the fourth chapel service. Usually, when something like that happens, they put the whole facility on lockdown and send the prisoners back to their cells.

This time, the guards decided not to implement the lockdown. I'd been praying for God's favor as the chaplain from the minimum side and I walked back to the medium control booth before the scheduled service. Amazingly, the guards allowed us through. Most of the time, they give you a body alarm to wear in case of emergency, but that day, none of the guards issued me one. The chaplain assured me that it would be fine because I'd always be close to someone with an alarm, and he sent me ahead to the meeting room while he finished his preparation.

Why hadn't they given me a body alarm? There was just a stabbing!

The fear I felt as I walked into the prison that first day tried to creep back. But I felt excitement and anticipation that God must have had something powerful planned for that night.

The sounds of my footsteps echoed through the tile corridors, and I tried not to look terrified. My heart pounded, and my palms grew slick with sweat as I realized that without God's help, I'd fall flat on my face. I nervously adjusted my clothing, took a deep breath and went into the meeting room.

There were a couple volunteers in there, as well as 20 or so prisoners milling around, each one clad in the uniform blues — t-shirts with jeans and denim jackets that screamed "State of Oregon, Department of Corrections" in orange letters. Grizzled, hardened faces turned to look at the sound of my entrance.

Tattooed arms reached out. "Come on, let's pray over here." Then 10 guys led me into the next room two doors away from anyone able to hear me scream for help. There were a bunch of metal chairs scattered around, and they sat me down in one. My eyes darted around, looking for the closest exit as the prisoners grabbed chairs for themselves, pulling them into a tight circle around me. I realized that the volunteers who wore body alarms were nowhere in sight.

"Let's pray."

I wondered if I needed to keep my eyes open as we prayed. I watched as every guy in the room bowed his head and folded his hands on his knees. I just stared at the carpet and 10 sets of white prison-issue sneakers and listened in amazement as they prayed for my safety. It was a prayer of protection, but it wasn't for the prison — it was for my drive home, through the sleet and the snow.

As the men prayed for me and also for the coming service and the prisoner who'd been stabbed, God told me not to worry.

These are my warriors, he told me, *and they're your brothers. You're safe.*

YOU WILL BE SCORCHED

The power of God fell heavily on that service. Afterward, I drove through hail, sleet, snow and fogged-over slippery roads, but none of it affected me. I didn't slide or skid once. The peace I felt as I thought about the power of the men's prayers was incredible. I knew none of the hazards of the road would touch me. It felt like I was being carried on the wings of angels, speeding to safety in the arms of God.

It's just where I've always been.

THE MIRACLE GIRL
The Story of
Jessica (Glaspie) Devore
Written by James Werning

It's strange to think of me doing something as exciting as taking two helicopter rides in one day and not remembering a thing about it. No wonder, though, since I was more dead than alive at the time. There's a little article on the Air Life of Oregon Web site that tells the story of my accidental shooting with a hunting pistol and how Air Life flew me to the hospital. The article ends with, "Jessica endured hours of surgeries and months of rehab, but she finally made a full recovery — something doctors attribute largely to her speedy emergency transport."*

Yes, my family and I are *extremely* grateful to Air Life for their part in saving my life. The medical personnel were so amazing. But that's just one part of a larger story. Thankfully, I get to tell the *full story* here, which includes one incredible miracle after another. People call me the miracle girl!

***

Sunday, October 6, 2002.

It was the perfect day. Or so I thought. At 12 years of age, there was nothing I liked better than camping and hunting with my extended family in the mountains. I loved everything about it: the huge ponderosa pines, all our trailers circled around a big campfire, a tribe of cousins to roam with, rocks to climb, forts to build, the enormous blue sky, the scent of pine in the air. It was all so wonderful. That particular day was unseasonably warm. Grandpa Bob had just finished an open-air church service — he was the preacher in the family. Then we kids got to go shooting under the supervision of my cousin Shannon, who was 24.

We wanted to drive down a dirt road to go shooting, but Shannon said, "No. Let's just stay here around camp." So we strolled down the dirt road in the warm sunshine, shooting as we walked.

Pretty soon, I was out of ammo so I asked another cousin, "Hey, Matt. Will you load my rifle for me?"

He said, "Sure. You can shoot my pistol while I load yours." So I took his .22 pistol.

After shooting a couple times, I heard a shot, and I felt something. Immediately, I knew I'd been hit, although I didn't feel any pain and didn't see any blood. To this day, I don't know how I did it. But I had shot myself in the stomach — just above my belly button.

"Mason, I've been shot!" I shouted to another cousin. Then I got really weak and fell to the ground.

At first, Shannon thought I was joking because we were always playing tricks on her. But Mason kept yelling, "No, really, she's been shot!" I remember just looking at the sky and finding it really hard to think clearly. My thoughts quickly became cloudy and confused.

Shannon gently set my head in her lap and said, "Look at me, baby. Please look at me!" The last thing I remember were the tears in her eyes.

The tears.

Then I blacked out.

***

We found out later that the bullet had bounced all around my abdomen. It seriously damaged my intestines, my colon and my appendix, and it eventually lodged in my left pelvis. But that's not the worst of it. The bullet hit my aorta twice. Doctors say I should have been dead in minutes because of that fatal injury.

When I fell to the ground, my cousins started screaming and crying for help. My parents heard the shouts back at the camp. Somebody said I had been shot, so my dad took off running. He sprinted about 25 yards, and suddenly, he stopped. My father actually heard God telling him to turn around and get the car. That was a good thing because I was bleeding to death, and every second counted. So Dad got the car and sped the quarter mile to where I'd been shot. As he arrived, he saw a man, a stranger, kneeling beside my body. Nobody knew who this man was or where he had come from.

The peculiar thing is that afterward, when everyone compared notes, they all remembered this man in different ways. Some swore he was wearing camouflage. Others said he was wearing hunter's orange. Still others said he had regular jeans and a t-shirt. Nobody remembers his facial features — not the slightest detail. They saw his white truck sitting there, but nobody saw him come, and nobody saw him go. That alone is astounding, considering there is only one way into that area, and it's right past our camp. That little camp is on a rocky knoll so remote, it's rare if even one vehicle comes by on any given day. But nobody saw this vehicle come or go. We did everything we could to locate him in the following months — we even put a notice on the radio, but we couldn't find him. I call him my angel.

My dad had picked me up and was holding me, asking, "Who will go with me?" The man took me from my dad and started to get in the back seat, but at the same time, my cousin Josiah was getting in on the other side, so he handed my nearly lifeless body to Josiah and off we sped. I can't imagine the fear in his heart as he knew that I could die in his arms. It's probably good I wasn't awake because Dad tells me he broke all land speed records on that trip.

Meanwhile, everyone back at the camp gathered around the campfire and started praying. They say it was unlike any prayer time they'd ever experienced. Everyone called out to God at once, pleading for my life with heart and soul. My dad and cousin were doing the same thing in the car. It makes me cry just thinking about how much everyone cared for me. To think about my mom who collapsed in the dirt when she heard about the shooting. To think about her tears and prayers, "Please … please, God, don't take my baby. Take me instead. I beg you." I've heard there's no greater pain on earth than that of a mother's broken heart.

People with aorta injuries like mine will typically bleed to death in 10 to 15 minutes. For me, it was 30 minutes before we even reached the ambulance that Uncle Kevin had summoned by cell phone. He was the only one who had a bag phone, and that was the only kind that has service in such a remote area. During that time, I actually stopped breathing three times. Each time, my dad stopped the car and rushed to where Josiah was holding me, thinking that resuscitation could bring me back. And each time, I gasped and started breathing again. They tell me it happened again in the ambulance, when I "died" several times and came back to life. They started putting fluid back into my veins during that 10-minute ambulance trip to La Pine, Oregon, but I was losing blood as fast as they could pump it in.

In La Pine, they transferred me to an Air Life helicopter and took off for Bend. Months later, my family returned and talked to the people who had helped me along the way. My mom even interviewed them on video, and their stories are absolutely incredible. The pilot on that flight remembers hearing the nurse in back praying as she worked on me. They weren't quiet little prayers, either. She prayed as if she were in the middle of battle — loud and furious. While she was tending my wounds, she cried out, "God, you can't take her now! This girl has a purpose for you on earth. We won't let her go. She's got to make it, God. Don't take her now!"

Tears streamed down the seasoned pilot's face as he told us that I died three more times in the helicopter. He recalled the mother tiger defending her cub. She firmly believed God wanted to save my life. She was not alone. My dad was begging for a miracle when God said to him, "I've already performed a miracle." Wow, it makes me wonder if some kind of invisible battle was being fought for my life.

Nobody at Saint Charles Medical Center had much hope for me when we landed in Bend. I had completely flat-lined. That was about an hour after I had been shot. I should not have lived even 15 minutes, but thank God I did. Nevertheless, they rushed me into surgery and opened me up from sternum to pelvis to try and fix the critical injuries to my aortic artery. One doctor actually held his fingers on the holes in my artery while another doctor harvested a vein from my leg. They used that vein to replace a section of my aorta. What a lovely scar it left behind. They found a horrible mess in there, but all the damage to my intestines and other organs would have to wait.

My relatives got to the hospital about that time. Then they received the shock of their lives when a nurse came out of my surgery and said, "Jessica's alive … barely." Most of them had no idea my condition was so bad.

My surgeon in Bend, Dr. Archer, said, "If she makes it, we want to send her to a pediatric specialist."

My parents and grandparents were allowed to see me in the ICU, essentially to say goodbye. Shocked by the sight of my swollen face and tubes going down my throat and into my neck, arms and legs, my family struggled to recognize the Jessica they had always known. The ICU nurse put her arm around my mom and said, "Remember, you will have memories to hang on to." My mom did not want memories; she wanted me.

The surgeons left the incision in my abdomen open, as there was much more to repair inside of me. They packed it with saline-soaked gauze and wrapped me completely with what looked like a giant bubble wrap blanket to keep my temperature from dropping too low. The doctors advised flying me to Portland, Oregon's Doernbecher Children's Hospital, where I would get the best possible care as soon as I was stable and should I survive, which was still unlikely. My parents agreed.

So I was flown to Portland for another surgery late Sunday night. That's when they removed half my colon, some intestine and my appendix. My parents drove to Portland that night, making a quick stop at our home, which was right off the highway. They picked up a change of clothes, a toothbrush and my favorite teddy bear. My mom says she just stood in my room for a moment thinking, *We might be coming back home without Jessica. I could never go back in this room. I could not bear it.* I can't imagine how horrible that must have been for her and Dad.

My prognosis in Portland was fatal. With a sober countenance, one of the doctors, who had even worked in a major inner-city hospital, said, "I've seen a lot of gunshot injuries before, but I've never seen one as bad as Jessica's."

There was a collective gasp as the chill of this cold reality began to set in.

I received 24 pints of blood that first day, when the average capacity of a girl my age is less than eight pints. The doctors said that if the aortic injury didn't kill me, then the peritonitis would. This is a bad, bad infection that happens when bowels are severed. Miraculously, that infection never developed, which is very, very rare. My story is one miracle after another.

Everyone who had the medical experience and knowledge told my family that I would probably die. And the doctors were absolutely right, based on probabilities. Meanwhile, my family was holding on to the promises Dad and others had received: "I've already performed a miracle." God said it, so they believed it, as crazy as it seemed.

My family sent out calls and e-mails to everyone they knew. The call for prayer literally went around the world. They even put the request for prayer on a local radio station. My parents saw immediate answers to those prayers as the doctors upgraded my condition from critical to serious on Monday. "Her progress is astounding," they said. But I didn't know any of that. I was in a drug-induced coma until the middle of the week.

After we had been in Portland a few days, someone asked my mom, "What if insurance doesn't cover all this?" The bills from the hospital in Bend alone totaled $65,000, not to mention the months of treatment that would likely follow.

THE MIRACLE GIRL

Without hesitation, my mom responded. "If we lose our house, we'll live in our little camp trailer. My daughter is more important than all our stuff." Mom said it only took one gunshot to get all her priorities in order.

***

Slowly, I regained consciousness. My eyes weren't even open when bursts of excruciating pain shot through my chest. I could hardly breathe! Strange smells and the sound of machines assaulted my senses. I opened my eyes to bright and blurry lights. I felt knives in my arms and side — I discovered a thicket of tubes and needles. I struggled not to gag on a tube down my throat. I gasped, "What's going on? What happened?" My mom said I'd been shot, and then I remembered. I told them I'd done it myself accidentally, so they wouldn't think any of my cousins had done it. Then I slipped out of consciousness again.

I was in and out a lot those first few days. Later, they tried to get me up and walking, which was incredibly difficult. The only things worse than the pain were two bags, which were my constant companions, attached by tubes to my colon and small intestine. They were called a colostomy and an ileostomy. The doctors actually left my incision open the entire three weeks I was in the hospital in Portland.

I struggled emotionally a lot those days. *Why is this happening to me?* I'd cry out to God.

It was more suffering than I thought a little girl should have to endure. *What did I do to deserve this?* I'd just cry and cry.

My mom and dad were a big encouragement, and they never left me the whole time. My extended family was incredible. There were as many as 80 friends and relatives in the waiting room while I was in surgery, and the staff said they'd never seen that before. I have an amazing family, and that really helped get me through. Someone I barely knew went to Outback Steak House and brought back a horde of good food for my family. Of course, all I could do was look at it because I wasn't allowed to touch a crumb of real food. But it was still a huge blessing for my family. Many of our friends went out of their way to help us during that difficult time.

Finally, I was well enough to go home, but only for a few weeks until I could return for another surgery. Boy, did I hate those colostomy and ileostomy bags! We had to change them night and day and take them everywhere I went. Walking was extremely painful. Gradually, it got better, but unfortunately, my hobbling journeys took me to a mirror. Ugh! What a hideous creature I found there! I gasped to discover a skinny little waif buried in a bundle of pajamas about four sizes too big for her. The greasy tuft of hair on top was a ratted mess. And this was me! Cautiously, I lifted a corner of my pajama top to take a peek at my stomach. The huge scar crushed my hopes of ever looking normal again. Or pretty. I felt such defeat and depression.

Meanwhile, I was a prisoner in my own home. All I could do was watch TV. I didn't have the motivation for crafts or hobbies or anything more interesting.

My big goal was to get rid of my bags by my 13th birthday, which was December 22. But first I needed surgery to reconnect my intestines. We returned to Portland in early December where they opened me up again. Of course, that meant a lot more pain and suffering and wires and tubes down my nose. But thankfully, the surgery was successful. Then I had to retrain myself to do all sorts of fun things like eat real food and go to the bathroom. I'd been without food for so long that everything tasted gross and disgusting.

I still struggled with my weight but even more with those awful, repulsive scars. I believed my weight would return one day, but I knew the scars could never change. Meanwhile, my pitiful resentment grew like cancer. I could see no possible good in this whole situation. All my questions for God seemed to hit the ceiling and fall right back down. My anger and disillusionment grew day by day. All I could think of was poor pitiful me.

***

I always loved being around other kids my age. But my parents homeschooled me, and that left me feeling isolated. My dad knew how I felt, so when I was unconscious, he told me he'd let me go to public school if I lived through this ordeal. When I woke up, I remembered what he said. One of the first things I asked him was if he meant what he said and if I could go to public school.

By the following September, I was well enough to attend eighth grade at the local school. Earlier, my friends told me how amazing public school was and how I would love it. It wasn't true for me. Actually, I hated it. The kids teased me for being so skinny. Then I'd compare myself to all those pretty girls with their perfect stomachs, and that made me just want to crawl in a hole and die. I would have quit school that September, but somehow I kept going.

I was doing better by the end of the year, but then things took a turn for the worse when I started high school. I started hanging out with the wrong crowd, and I got into trouble. When I was a freshman, my friend brought some alcohol to school. "Let's go out on the football field and drink," she said.

It was lunchtime, and I was feeling a bit ornery, so I said, "Sure." The next thing I knew, we were both drunk. Word quickly got around that I was drinking at school, so I actually had to confess to my parents. That was painful, especially since we were such a "holy" family. After all, my grandfather was a preacher, and we faithfully attended his church every Sunday. Each weekend, I sat quietly in church, and then each week, I got deeper into trouble. I started sneaking out at night and going to parties. At first, I thought, *Whoa! This is fun.* I was scared to death of getting caught, but it's not like my parents didn't know I was flirting with trouble. They made it clear they didn't like my friends. In the end, my parents were right.

I came to realize most of my friends weren't even true "friends." Alcohol was all we had in common. Most of them would gossip behind my back and cut me down to nothing. I suppose I stayed simply because it was the "cool" thing to do. What's more, I was seriously sick of the "good girl" reputation that was haunting me. I was sick of being the homeschooled girl from the perfect family who got good grades and never did anything wrong.

Then there was that "miracle girl" image I just couldn't shake. No matter where I went in my little town, I'd run into somebody who would say, "Oh, my! You're the little girl who got shot." That became my title: "The girl who got shot." After hearing that for two or three years, I would scream with rage inside. *That's not who I am! I am Jessica. I'm not the girl who got shot. I don't want to be known by that anymore.*

***

Eventually, I knew I needed to change. I simply got sick of the party scene. The "coolness" faded away, and I saw it for the unfulfilling lifestyle it really is. I took a good, hard look at these party people. I asked myself, *Are these the kind of people you really want to spend the rest of your life with? Do you want them to define your identity?* The answer was so clear to me. *No way! They're fakes. They hate each other. All they care about are the bottles in their hands. This is all a stupid waste of time.* So gradually, I became disgusted with the life I'd chosen.

About that time, we started attending a new church called Living Hope, and for the first time, I actually liked going to church! The things we discussed were relevant to my life. I loved going to youth group, and I liked being involved in the fun things that were happening there. More than anything, I was impressed at the way people actually loved each other and cared for each other.

Although I didn't stop partying overnight, I gradually moved in the opposite direction. One day, I went to one of my best friends and told him what I wanted to do.

"I don't want to party or drink anymore. So either you can stop partying, or we won't be able to see each other anymore."

His reaction really surprised me because I thought we were such good friends. He totally flipped out.

"Whatever! Are you too good for me or something? Fine, then. You go and hang out with all your church friends."

"No," I told him. "It's not like that. I just don't want to party anymore." He didn't get it, and neither did most of my other so-called friends. Some of them got really mad at me. Honestly, most of them didn't even care as long as they had their alcohol. I pray that someday they, too, will see the emptiness of that lifestyle and turn to the one who can fill the void as I did. Maybe my story will be the encouragement they need.

I've heard it said that when one door shuts, another one opens. Well, God opened a huge door for me with some really good Christian friends at that time. And the biggest blessing, by far, was my friend David. We had similar backgrounds, and we began walking together away from the party lifestyle. He helped me learn that being a Christian is more than just doing church stuff — it's living in a loving, obedient relationship with Jesus Christ. "Relationship" is the key word there.

A relationship happens when two people really care for each other, and that's how it was between God and me. When I was little, I thought I was a Christian by association: because of my Christian family and because of Grandpa Bob, the preacher. Today, I know I can't have a meaningful relationship with God if it is secondhand. I understand that God is *my* God. I speak with him; I walk with him; I live my life with him. This brings me so much happiness.

As for David, he totally swept me off my feet. We fell in love, and after graduating from high school, we married. David is such an incredible encouragement to me today, like when I'm tempted to crawl back into my cave of self-pity and resentment. He doesn't care about my scars. I'm beautiful to him, and he loves me unconditionally. He's helped me see how all of the stuff that happened to me can actually be helpful to others. I no longer cringe at my "miracle girl" reputation. I see how God has created each one of us for an incredibly wonderful purpose. If God miraculously spared me from death so I could help others, then so be it.

I'm just thrilled he would choose me for any purpose at all!

***

Less than a year after my accident, Grandpa Bob called the family together. He decided we should all go back to our hunting camp to give thanks to God. He said we should create a lasting monument to God's miraculous healing power. So we went there in July of 2003 — about 40 of us. Everyone went out in the forest and collected rocks. Then we piled them in a heap, cemented them together and attached a plaque to the top. It's still out there in the forest today. The plaque reads:

Joshua 4:21b, 24: "What are these stones? That all may know the mighty hand of the Lord and fear the Lord God forever."

On October 6, 2002, 12-year-old Jessica Glaspie was accidentally shot. She received fatal injuries, but through what could only be a miracle from God and many amazing people in the 911 system from the sheriff's department, La Pine EMTs, Air Life, Saint Charles Medical Center and Doernbecher's emergency room staff and surgeons, she survived.

Psalm 30:2-3, 12: "O Lord our God, we cried out to you, and you healed Jessica; you brought her soul from the grave. You kept her alive. O Lord our God, we give you thanks forever!"

We dedicate this site to the Glory of God!

***

Just recently, I was talking to a man who is really into hunting, and I told him a little bit about my story. I do that from time to time these days, and if people are lucky, I'll even show them my scars. This guy was astounded.

"Whoa!" he said. "Did that really happen to you?"

It's so amazing that every single doctor said there's no way I should have survived. And to think of all the people who were wrestling in prayer with every ounce of strength they could possibly muster; to think of the "angel" who showed up to help me and the promise given to my dad; to think of a doctor who would reach inside me just to hold my life blood in his hand; to think that I didn't get the infections everyone said I should get; to think of that nurse in the helicopter who prayed over me like a mother tiger defending her cub. Not to mention all the times I died and then came back. I can't think of a word besides "miraculous" to describe it all. I suppose I really am the miracle girl!

*www.airlife.org/PatientStories_glaspie.html

HEALING HANDS
THE STORY OF MICHELLE
WRITTEN BY ELLEN R. HALE

Exhaustion overwhelmed me as I plodded through my work at the Bureau of Indian Affairs in Portland, Oregon. I struggled to keep from dozing off. I had been partying more than usual in the wake of my 21st birthday, but that alone didn't explain my tiredness.

A positive pregnancy test made it perfectly clear.

From the time I was a child, I had loved babies and knew I wanted to be a mother someday. But I wasn't prepared to be a single mother. That's why I had been on birth control for several years. Even though I stopped for a short time, I mistakenly thought I'd be protected from pregnancy.

Because I wanted a man to love me so badly, I had been with three different guys that month. My mind reeled over the decision I needed to make. I asked for two weeks off from work, and my sister and I escaped on a road trip to Arizona to discuss my options.

"You know I always wanted to have babies," I told my sister. "But not this way."

"Michelle, I'll support you no matter what you choose," she assured me. "You'll have help if you keep the baby."

By the time we returned, I had come to a decision. I always did what I wanted, and this would be no different. I would have this baby on my own, doing all I could to be my child's mother *and* father.

***

Growing up near the Warm Springs Indian Reservation, I was the third of four children born to my white mother and my Colville Indian father. Our family attended Catholic Mass in Latin every week, but the services puzzled me. As a child, I quoted prayers but didn't understand many of the words I recited. Since we were taught the priest was the only one who could speak directly to God, I thought I had to go to him whenever I had a prayer request. I don't remember our family ever talking about God outside church.

My parents divorced when I was 16, and I stayed with my mother. Somehow, I graduated from high school in 1972, despite skipping class all the time. From the outside, my life appeared perfect. My classmates voted me homecoming princess two times. I was a cheerleader and always had boyfriends.

But inside, depression dragged me down. I knew in my head that my parents loved me, but I never felt loved. I especially resented my father after the divorce. Suicidal thoughts constantly invaded my mind. *No one loves me. I'm worthless.*

Alcohol was a regular presence in the family when I was older. Family members drank when celebrating holidays and birthdays and when going on hunting trips. They would drink and drive without hesitation. If someone visited our home, we offered him or her a beer.

The drinking sometimes led to danger. I was partying with my older brother and sister when her husband came in drunk, which set off a fight. My brother-in-law threatened to hurt both of my siblings. Scared and desperate, I called on neighbors for help. After the situation calmed down, we all passed out from drunkenness. This was just the beginning of alcohol bringing violent times into my life.

***

When I moved to Portland, I lived as a functioning alcoholic. Since I didn't know many people, I hit the bars every weekend looking for love in all the wrong places. I deeply wanted to feel loved, but I settled for the illusion of love that came when someone slept with me. The rejection that soon followed added layer after layer to my depression.

When I found out I was pregnant and determined to be the best single mom ever, I quit drinking but didn't give up my social life. I gave birth to a beautiful baby girl in 1976.

My first year with Nicole was a dream come true. I stayed home with her and lived on welfare.

Seeking guidance, I read all the parenting magazines I could. I loved dressing up my daughter in cute outfits. I expected her to behave perfectly since that would show everyone I was the perfect mother.

But every weekend, I drank with my friends. In my heart, I desperately wanted to find the love of my life who would marry me. I desired to be a stay-at-home mom, caring for my family. We could be a normal family.

When I went out, I left Nicole with anyone who would watch her — a teenage babysitter or my father, even though I knew he'd probably be drinking while he watched her.

Around Nicole's 2nd birthday, all the pressure I put on myself turned me into a simmering teakettle about to wail. When Nicole cried too much or spilled her milk, feelings of pure rage filled my body. I spit out burning words for minutes on end.

"You stupid little b****!" I screamed. "What did you do that for? Why didn't you listen to me? You never do what I say!"

The more she cried, the more I belittled her. If I had a hangover, Nicole's screams pierced my pounding head. I yelled until she crumbled.

"Shut up! Just shut up!"

Many times, I came close to physically hurting her. That's when I made an appointment with a counselor. I knew I wasn't being a good mother. Like all the counseling I had at various times since I was a teenager, it didn't seem to help. Nothing filled the void of hopelessness in my heart.

***

HEALING HANDS

A few summers later, I began seriously dating someone whom I had met in a bar. By the fall, we decided to have a baby together. But the relationship quickly turned unstable, and I left him because he drank too much. I was on my own again.

As soon as my second daughter, Keeley, was born in 1981, I returned to the only lifestyle I knew — usually working two jobs to make ends meet during the week, then partying to escape the stress of my life on the weekends. I never considered that if I didn't have to pay babysitters to watch the girls when I went out, I wouldn't have needed a second job.

As my girls grew, I began to talk to them about avoiding drugs, doing well in school and living right. I involved them in activities like swimming, dancing and softball. But they saw my life clearly for what it was — an endless cycle of failed relationships and nights wasted away by drinking. My actions spoke louder than my words.

My fits of rage happened less frequently. Instead, I felt dead inside. I sometimes hid in my bed all day with the curtains pulled shut. I didn't answer the phone; I didn't open the door. I had no idea what my girls did during those "black hole" days. I thought about killing myself only to realize I had to keep living to care for my girls.

***

I stepped into the medical clinic in Prineville with yet another boy and waited for the doctor. I was pregnant again, and this time, I decided to have an abortion.

I had rationalized this decision: I didn't want to have my boyfriend's baby because he smoked pot and never held a job long; I couldn't handle raising another child on my own; I didn't want another child to experience my anger problems.

Even though my boyfriend was a deadbeat, our on-again, off-again relationship lasted 10 years. When I had another unplanned pregnancy, I didn't even tell him. I just returned to the clinic and had another abortion. I rushed off on a camping trip so that my boyfriend wouldn't wonder why I was a complete wreck, crying all the time and bleeding from the abortion. No one ever knew, except one close girlfriend.

A new counselor I was seeing finally convinced me that I had enough strength to ditch my boyfriend. After that, I hooked up with another guy I met at a bar — another unplanned pregnancy, another abortion. My response had become automatic. *I can't even afford the kids I already have. I'm a horrible mother to them. I can't have another kid.*

Afterward, I decided to have another medical procedure so I could never get pregnant again. I didn't trust myself anymore.

***

I realized that children do as you do — not as you say — when my daughter Nicole confessed that she was pregnant. She was 15 years old. Her boyfriend was a few years older than she, and they were convinced they could handle parenting. But I immediately took responsibility for this child's wellbeing.

While Nicole dropped out of school, I returned to work for the federal government because the insurance would cover my daughter's pregnancy. After her son was born, she and her boyfriend found an apartment and moved in together. Her boyfriend only lasted three months before retreating home.

My heart broke seeing my daughter follow in my footsteps. I had put so much pressure on her to be a perfect child, not realizing my actions were teaching her to make the wrong choices.

I began to notice a change in Nicole's behavior. When I dropped in at her place, I found evidence of partying. Her attention to my grandson decreased. I stopped at her apartment to collect some of his belongings and found beer cans strewn everywhere. The electricity had been shut off. Soon I connected the dots and realized Nicole was using drugs. I tried to take care of my grandson every weekend so I knew he was safe.

I contacted Child Protective Services in an effort to obtain custody of my grandson, but they told me I didn't have enough proof of neglect.

The day I found him at my father's home with filthy clothes and raw buttocks, I rushed to show him to the authorities. They granted me custody of my 18-month-old grandson.

STRENGTH FOR TODAY

***

Much to my surprise, I also began to notice a change in Keeley's behavior. She was a really good kid, so I was worried when she started dating a boy who drank and used drugs. I feared she would experience the pain I had. Then she met Matt, who attended a church called Living Hope Christian Center. Keeley had become disinterested in attending Mass with me, but she woke up on her own every Sunday to go to Living Hope with Matt.

I was born a Catholic. I never considered attending other kinds of churches. Yet this church that Keeley enjoyed so much intrigued me. I wondered what kept her attending every week.

One Sunday morning, I accompanied Keeley and Matt to Living Hope. I immediately felt different, though I didn't know why. Something penetrated deep into my soul. Tears streamed down my face as the worship service progressed. God was touching me, healing me and cleansing me.

Week after week, I heard more about God's love for me, despite what I had done. Soon I was coming early for Sunday school, then coming back on Sunday evenings and Wednesday nights. God had slowly reeled me in like a floundering fish, and now I was in his loving hands. I was experiencing the love I had searched for my whole life.

I didn't realize how much I didn't know about the Bible and Christianity. It was an embarrassing position for an adult.

HEALING HANDS

I had never even truly understood the role of Jesus in Christmas and Easter! My grandson asked me simple questions about Jesus that I couldn't answer.

Matt gave me a Bible our first Christmas together. He even had my name engraved on the cover. I held the book like a foreign object that puzzled me. *This is a nice gift, but what am I going to do with it? I guess I'll carry it to church like everyone else does.*

It was several years before that Bible became my most valuable possession once I really started reading it and learned how to understand what it meant.

For the first year I attended Living Hope, every service left me in tears. Some were tears of sadness that I hadn't followed God's guidelines for living and had suffered the consequences. I grieved for the life I could have had if I had known God when I was growing up or when I was raising my children. I realized children have a hole in their lives without a godly father — God's plan for every family is for both parents to raise their children. I thought about my frustration over Nicole's drug addiction and wondered how much more God grieved over me, his child, repeating the same destructive behaviors over and over. He wanted better for me just like I wanted better for Nicole. I now saw how destructive decisions always affect the next generation.

Because I longed for cleansing from all my sins, I decided to be baptized in December 1998. My understanding was that after I accepted God's offer of salvation through faith in Christ, I would be washed clean. Therefore, my expectations for my baptism were high. When the pastor plunged me beneath the water and lifted me up, I blinked my eyes. *Why didn't I feel any different? I wanted to be a brand new person — all my anger replaced with kindness, gentleness and love. But I didn't feel washed clean at all!*

Eventually, I learned that baptism was just the first step in the long, sometimes difficult process of becoming all that God intended me to be.

***

When I saw Sarah at Living Hope, I glared at her in disdain. The church had given her family Christmas gifts while she had been in jail. *How dare she come here after all she's done!* I caught a glimpse of her raising her hands, praising God, and I burned with hatred toward her as my old tendency toward uncontrolled anger took hold.

Sarah shared drugs with Nicole, who practically worshipped Sarah and listened to whatever she said. I couldn't separate the two of them.

Now here was Sarah worshipping in my church. God had a plan and put us together face to face one Sunday in the foyer, and I wanted to rub it in her face that I had gotten Nicole into Teen Challenge, a Christian residential recovery center for drug addicts.

Instead, God softened my heart and told me to hug Sarah. We began crying together.

Afterward, I began picking her up for church services, trying to encourage and support her. We started studying the Bible together, but soon Sarah ended up in jail again. I visited her frequently and mailed a chapter of a Christian book to her each week. I saw her desire for God deepen.

When she started a Bible study with some other inmates, I began to suggest that she try Teen Challenge like Nicole. Sarah was adamantly opposed. Still, I kept visiting her.

"Guess what?" Sarah said with a smile.

"What?"

"I'm going to Teen Challenge in Portland," she replied.

"That's great! I'll start working on getting you into the program," I offered.

"I don't think God would have told me if I wasn't going," she assured me.

She was right. Sarah was quickly accepted into Teen Challenge.

***

Nicole and her three children were living 550 miles away in Missoula, Montana, when my phone rang, and I heard the scared voice of my 10-year-old grandson. Nicole was using again.

I don't know how I'll do it, but I have to rescue my grandchildren. I want Nicole to come with us, but we have to get the kids.

Sarah and another young woman agreed to make the trip with me. I frantically called anyone in Missoula who might help us — Child Protective Services, pastors and the parole officer of Nicole's current boyfriend, who had a criminal record.

I had suspected for months that Nicole was using again and agonized over what to do. I decided to trust God to show me if he wanted me to take action. God was telling me the time had come, but I was nervous about the impending confrontation. As we traveled through the frigid February day, we prayed aloud and played worship songs, depending on God the whole way.

We all knew Nicole would be high when we arrived. We sent Sarah into the apartment first, hoping that Nicole would listen to her.

"Why are you here?" I heard her ask Sarah. "Everything's fine."

"Things are not good, Nicole. Let me help you."

A few minutes later, she was screaming hysterically.

"Get out! You have no right to be here!"

Everyone tried to stay calm and compassionate, even though we repeatedly told her the children were leaving with us. Unfortunately, the meth in Nicole's body didn't allow her to hear our loving intentions. For the next 24 hours, Nicole lashed out at me before finally settling down and agreeing to come back to Madras with us. I headed to U-Haul to rent a trailer, and we packed up their belongings the next day. We needed to move quickly because we all had responsibilities back in Madras.

I didn't know how we'd make it back, though. It was snowing hard when we left Missoula. Only Nicole and I had driver's licenses. Withdrawal from her meth addiction slammed her hard. We drove for a while before having to pull over so Nicole could vomit. When she wouldn't stop vomiting, we were forced to find a place to stay.

Our money was running out, snow was falling harder, the kids were growing restless and the cramped SUV was uncomfortable. We stopped at a motel and held out a coupon book we picked up along the way. Generously, the manager gave all seven of us a suite for a price we could afford. I spent the night sobbing in the closet with a flashlight, reading a Christian book and searching for Bible verses to give me hope. I didn't want the children to know how terrified and distraught I was.

When we awoke in the morning, more than a foot of snow had accumulated. I didn't have money to buy chains for the SUV or the U-Haul, so I prayed God would keep us safe. *Lord, we're starting out now because I know you will take care of us since I have no more money to wait out the storm.* An hour away from the motel, the snowstorm lifted and clear skies emerged — proof of God's timing.

***

After I began depending on God each day, he took away my need and desire for alcohol.

But locked away deep in my soul was guilt and shame that would not go away — the emotional scars from my abortions. The ugliness of what I had done festered inside me for years, affecting me without my knowledge. I had sought help from counselor after counselor, but not a single one ever asked me if I had an abortion. They pre-scribed antidepressants instead. But without identifying the root of my problems, we were unable to work on moving past them.

A woman at Living Hope told me about a retreat she attended on healing from abortion. She planned on offering the retreat in her home and invited me to come. I hesitantly accepted, wanting to rid myself of the secret I held inside.

That weekend was one of the most painful of my life. The small group of women and I recalled in excruciating detail what happened to our aborted children, who were not disposable fetuses but living human beings. I had blocked the truth from my mind to the extent that, before that weekend, I had forgotten about the third abortion. I was disgusted with myself for the selfish reasons I conjured up for killing my babies. With one of the pregnancies, I was sick so intensely that I figured something was wrong with the baby. I hated reliving the events I covered up for so many years.

Weeks later, I was able to fully repent for what I had done. I overflowed with gratitude toward God for making me alive again.

Everyone at Living Hope has helped my faith increase. Most importantly, I have witnessed the power of prayer. Before Living Hope, I didn't even know I could talk directly to God.

At a time when my daughter was using drugs, a friend of hers called me and told me she had used the previous evening. If I wanted to turn her into the police, her friend assured me the drugs would still be in her bloodstream. I called her parole officer but received no response. I was pacing and praying intensely when there was a knock on my door. It was one of the Christian mentors God had placed in my life!

"Did I forget an appointment we had?" I asked, wiping tears from my face.

"No, Michelle," she said. "I was driving through town when God told me to come see you. So, what's going on?"

I choked out the latest development with Nicole as she came inside to pray with me. Before coming to Living Hope, I never had anyone to turn to in crisis who would lead me to God for help.

One of the many times I was caring for Nicole's three children, I became very ill and couldn't work at my massage therapy business. I stood at the kitchen sink worrying about how I would feed the kids when I noticed the birds flying around outside.

God put the words of Matthew 6:26 in my mind. "Look at the birds of the air. They do not sow or reap or store away in barns, and yet your heavenly father feeds them. Are you not much more valuable than they?"

Of course God will take care of us.

Sure enough, some of my clients stopped by and gave us money and food.

***

STRENGTH FOR TODAY

At church, I have also learned about the importance of being a parent who knows God and the importance of a father's role in the family — something my girls didn't experience. Parents can't wait until their kids are grown up or until they've made some bad decisions before bringing God into their lives. That's why I've used every opportunity to teach my grandchildren to pray all the time — when they get hurt or when they're having a bad day. Instead of teaching them to run to drugs or alcohol, I want them to run to God.

The first time I shared my story with our church was during a Mother's Day service. The pastor handed me the microphone, and I shared my whole story. I warned of the severe repercussions of abortion. When I chose abortion, I never imagined how negatively the decision would impact me. I closed my talk with a challenge for mothers.

Father, for years I have wanted to speak out to young women and share my testimony with them in hopes that they would not go down the same hard road that I did. God, I want to say a blessing over every mother here today. I pray for the strength to get up each day and do the best they can do in your name. I pray that they begin to know how long, how wide, how deep your love is for them. I pray that your love be overflowing so that it overflows to their children and others. You love us so much that you trust us with the gift of motherhood. You thought so much of us and are counting on us to raise our children up in the way that you desire; so, Father, I am praying that you will be obvious in our lives. We love you. Amen.

HEALING HANDS

After the service, I felt relief and wanted to jump for joy. I felt God's forgiveness — the forgiveness I'd been learning about. Several women who had abortions spoke to me, and I offered them advice on how to repent like I had. I had never enjoyed Mother's Day as much as that one — a Sunday I could truly celebrate.

***

My father, now in his 80s, has chronic lung disease. I moved in with him to help care for him after tiring of keeping up with both of our houses.

I continue to struggle with honoring my father as the Bible commands us to do. His alcoholism affected all of his children, even though he would never acknowledge that. He still drinks daily. When I see him pop open a can of beer, I flash back to all the negative repercussions of drunkenness I've witnessed in my life. It's hard to forgive him because he still has a drinking problem. But my love for God compels me to honor my earthly father.

My father takes oxygen all day, in addition to other treatments and medications. He becomes short of breath after walking just a few feet. I know God wants me to be responsible for him and do all I can for him.

My mother died 13 years ago, but we had been estranged ever since she moved to Florida when I was in my 20s. Since I never felt love from her, I am even more grateful for God's love.

I've often wondered, angrily, why God didn't save me

earlier in life and spare me from all I endured because of what I did. Now I know that he desires us to seek him but gives us the choice. My children and I suffered because I made the wrong choices, but now we are changing the future of our family by following God.

My oldest grandson, whom I've raised many of his 16 years, has chosen to live with me and my father. His mother, Nicole, who has four other children, has been clean for many years now, but he prefers attending school here.

My grandson comes to Living Hope with me, and I tell him Jeremiah 29:11 is true for him: "'For I know the plans I have for you,' declares the Lord, 'plans to prosper you and not to harm you, plans to give you hope and a future.'" We have communion in my bedroom every morning to remember that Christ's death was for us.

Thank you, Jesus, for dying on the cross for us. Forgive us for the times we sinned against you yesterday. Give us a clean heart, and bless us this day. Amen.

I have been self-employed as a massage therapist for the last 22 years. Massage therapy allows me to do what I love and pray all day long. In recent years, I have been asking God to work through me in the lives of my clients and be present in each session.

I attended a conference about bringing God into the workplace. Since then, I've been meeting weekly for Bible study with my daughter Keeley — who went on to marry Matt and works as a real estate agent — her friend and a friend of mine who operates a spa. We're striving to make

HEALING HANDS

God the CEO of our businesses, depending on him to provide financially for us and praying that he will give us opportunities to minister to others.

My clients range in age from teens to 94. Some have chronic headaches; some have severe back pain. Most of them know about my faith and my strong belief that God hears our prayers for physical and spiritual healing. If they don't know, I pray that God will open the door and allow me to speak about him or pray with them. I'm not shy about my relationship with Jesus. I let God set the scene by having Christian books out and available for them to take if they choose.

God has answered my prayers by using me in awesome ways.

As I massaged one woman's feet, I played worship music and sang along softly. I switched to instrumental music for the remainder of the massage so I could pray for her and her upcoming surgery. The presence of God filled the room.

"I'm afraid, Michelle," my client confessed afterward. "Will you keep me in prayer?"

"How about we pray together right now?" I suggested.

She nodded her head, and I guided her to a quiet room where we could talk to God. I've experienced his healing and know that anyone who turns to Jesus can be healed, too. When I returned to my studio, I gazed at the picture of Jesus on my wall. A man kneels before him, and Jesus, the great physician, touches him with his healing hands.

GOD'S PRINCESS
THE STORY OF SARAH
WRITTEN BY ARLENE SHOWALTER

"Can't you turn those things down?" Brian growled, wrapping a pillow around his ears. "Why are the scanners shrieking at this hour, anyway?"

I dashed out of our bedroom toward the first of our three police scanners. Just as my fingers touched the dial, the front door burst open, the officer's booted foot still in mid-air from his kick.

"Police! Freeze!" he ordered with his gun trained on me. I looked through the windows beyond him. Officers swarmed the front yard and surrounded the house.

As I heard the all-too-familiar click of handcuffs, my heart dropped to my toes. Busted again. Busted with a new twist; I was pregnant with my third child.

Mom's Knight

Our fairytale life began when Mom met Joe, a highly successful businessman. My 4-year-old heart found plenty to impress me. Joe owned every man-toy imaginable: speed and fishing boats, trailers, campers, cars and motor-cycles.

Joe gave Mom and me everything we could want — and more. Happy she hooked up with a man who could provide for all our physical needs, Mom worked hard for

Joe, both in his house and at his businesses.

Joe's intelligence and savvy helped him build two booming businesses. He owned a custom paint and body shop and a custom motorcycle shop.

"Sarah," Mom called up to me. "The latest catalog just arrived. Come on down, and let's look for school clothes," she continued as I bounced down the stairs, laughing gently as she brushed my shiny hair out of my eyes. "You are growing like a weed! I'm so glad I found Joe. He takes good care of us, doesn't he?" she added.

"Oh, yes! I'm glad, too. He said we'd all get snowmobiles this Christmas. I can't wait," I said, my happy feet dancing around the kitchen table.

"Oh, this is so cool," Mom exclaimed, pointing at a chic pants outfit and turning the catalog for me to see it better. She never even glanced at the price.

For hours, we shopped in the warmth and comfort of our cozy castle — Joe's big, beautiful secluded house.

But the magic castle was surrounded by a moat of distrust and fear. Distrust in all authority and fear of an invasion. Surrounded by the safety of our little world, I knew not to trust anyone on the "outside." I had no friends, no confidantes.

"Hey, Joyce." Joe came home all excited. "I bought a camper today. My hunting buddies are going out this weekend. Get it ready to go."

"That's so much work, and I only have two days to prepare," my mom protested.

"Just do it, and make sure everything is done right."

GOD'S PRINCESS

Joe looked hard at my mom.

On Friday, Joe picked up some other kids on our way to the camping area. They hopped into the camper with me.

"Joe, slow down," my mom said as we turned onto a dirt road. He ignored her. We kids got tossed around like ping-pong balls while he veered around sharp turns and flew over the rough dirt road.

"Joe, slow down! The kids are falling all over the camper!" she yelled.

He just laughed and hit the gas harder.

We finally arrived at the campsite. The place was flooded with guys out looking for a good time. As day darkened to night, they began to drink. The more they drank, the louder they got.

Guns appeared from nowhere. Unseen phantoms became targets as they fired their guns into the air. I huddled in my sleeping bag, trying to block the noise with fingers in my ears, too terrified to sleep.

Mom was my fairy godmother. She loved me with all her heart. She worked hard. My safety, comfort and needs were always her first concerns. She had moved in with Joe so her little princess could live the good life.

Our Night

Curious as to why Joe and his friends constantly sniffed white stuff into their noses, I decided to find out for myself. I took my Baby Alive doll's food and, with careful determination, chopped it up exactly as I'd watched Joe do many times.

"Here we go, baby." I demonstrated my new skill. "First, we have to chop this until it's powder, just like the grownups do.

"Now, I need to use this razor blade I found in the trash," I confided to Baby Alive. "Okay, careful now." I held my tongue between my teeth in concentration. "Gotta make this line straight, just like Joe does."

At last, the line of powder met with my 9-year-old approval. "Okay, baby, now we sniff it quickly through this straw, and then we will be super happy like Joe gets."

Quickly, I inhaled the powdered toy food, burning my nasal passage. "Ew, that's gross," I sputtered. "Whatever does Joe see in that? Why does he like it so much?"

A dragon had penetrated our secure castle. His name was Speed. Soon, he invited Methamphetamines to join his destructive crusade. They took over and conquered our little kingdom.

Joe had worked hard at his two businesses, building a reputation as the best detail person around. Mom worked the offices for him, without pay.

"Joe can't make it today." Mom hastened to soothe an irate customer. "He's waiting for a part that hasn't come in yet."

"Joe's sick today. He'll finish your bike tomorrow."

"You didn't get your payment? I'm sure it's in the mail."

Mom dodged angry clients and persistent creditors

with the skill of a prizefighter, while Joe sank deeper and deeper into addiction. He cared nothing about his reputation, business, employees or family.

Work slowed to a trickle. Employees were let go because Joe couldn't make payroll. His toys began to melt away under the heat of repossession or to pay outstanding debt.

Joe had flipped the "American Dream," sliding from riches to rags. He didn't care. Nothing mattered to him except his next rush of meth.

Mom struggled with weight issues, so she took a little speed to control it. Soon she had passed her fetish on to me.

"Stand up straight," she admonished. "Suck in your tummy. Watch what you eat. You don't want to be fat, do you?"

By 11, I was sneaking speed myself to keep my own preteen weight down. Nobody noticed because they were too busy using themselves. Pills lay all over the house, tucked into drawers, lying on the counter, at the office — a pill popper's paradise.

"Mom, I need some speed."

"You're 13. What do you want speed for?" she asked.

"I need to keep my weight down."

"Well, okay, if it's only for that, I guess it can't hurt. I don't want you to suffer being overweight as I have."

With one fateful announcement, our fairytale life began its final collapse.

"Joe, I'm pregnant," Mom announced when I was 14.

"Pregnant?" Joe roared, glazed eyes blazing. "How could you be so stupid? You know I don't like kids. I've only put up with yours 'cause she's smart enough to stay outta my way." He stumbled toward the bedroom, sitting heavily on rumpled sheets.

"How're we gonna afford another brat? How?" he demanded.

***

"Jenna and I are going to a sleepover tonight," I told Mom. "Is that okay?"

"Well, I guess so. Remember my baby shower is tomorrow afternoon. You need to be there."

"I will. I promise."

I ran out the door with Jenna. "Did she buy it?" she asked.

"Sure did. I'm ready to party."

Rather than an innocent sleepover, we had arranged to meet some boys for an all-nighter. One singled me out and began making clumsy sexual advances. I managed to fend him off, staying awake by popping diet pills.

Finally, as the first fingers of dawn brushed the horizon, I gave in. Then I stumbled into the shower to wash away the event, where I passed out.

"Sarah, are you okay?!" Jenna screamed in fear, slapping my face. "Sarah, talk to me."

"Huh?" I muttered in a deep fog. "I feel sick."

Jenna dragged me to the toilet, propping up my limp

head. I threw up with such violence, I felt surely my guts would follow. I laid my hot cheek against the cooling porcelain.

"What happened?" Jenna gasped.

"Must've been those diet pills. I don't know how many I took trying to keep Billy's hands outta my pants."

"Did you succeed?"

"Nah. He's gross."

My good friend Steve joined us in the bathroom. "Are you okay, Sarah?" Genuine concerned colored his words.

"Yeah, I'll be fine. I gotta be at Mom's baby shower at 2:00."

"Don't worry. I'll take care of you, I promise."

I arrived on time, and Mom never knew I lost my innocence and almost my life in one night.

Desperate Deals

Two months after Sissy's birth, Joe continued his tirade. "I've told you and told you I don't like kids. Get out. All of you."

"We're leaving," I yelled back. "Come on, Mom, get your stuff, and let's leave this hell hole."

Mom and I found a string of apartments. The three of us moved into one. Her older sister and child moved next door. Another sister, along with her husband and four children, moved on the other side. Having so much family close should have been cozy, but in reality, the apartments were horrible dirt holes.

Alone for the first time in 10 years, Mom had a 2-month-old infant and 14-year-old daughter to support and no means to do so. She had worked for Joe without pay.

Joe's biker buddies came to Mom's rescue, despising him for throwing her out with no income. They set her up in the only business they knew and understood — selling drugs.

Mom hated surviving this way. When she got busted six years later, she never used or sold drugs again. She found legitimate work and raised my sister beautifully.

I convinced my mother to allow me to live with a lady and her son, under the pretense of helping the lady out. In reality, I wanted to party without adult supervision or disapproval. Joe's dragon had its claws in me.

Starting on diet pills at 11, moving on to speed to control weight, it was only a matter of time before methamphetamines knocked their ugly claws on my door.

My Knight and Daze

"Hey, gorgeous, what's your name?" The tall guy grinned down at me, his golden locks brushing the black leather of his jacket.

"Hi. I'm Sarah."

"I'm Pat."

"You go to school around here?" I asked.

"Just graduated McClelland, over in Meyersville."

"McClelland? Never heard of it."

"Of course you haven't. It's some hoity-toity finishing school my folks insisted I go to." His easy laugh settled my curiosity. I believed him.

I learned too late that McClelland was a detention center, and my new guy was no knight in shining black leather. He was just a black knight, and at 15, I was carrying his child. I quit school, and we moved in together.

"Pat," I said, "I'm not staying with you unless you get a job or go into the service. We're going nowhere fast, and we have a baby on the way."

The military turned Pat down, so he found a job working on a ranch. While he was at work, someone knocked on our front door.

"Are you Sarah?"

"Yes, I am."

"Detective Jones." The man flashed his badge. "I have some questions. You know Pat Thompson?"

"Yes," I answered, swallowing hard. "What's wrong?"

"He just shot a guy six times in the face and left him for dead. He used the guy's car for his getaway. Any idea where he might be headed?"

"Please, can I call my mom?" My voice and hands shook.

"Go ahead, miss."

Mom and I learned Pat was on his way to our dealer friend's house in Eugene, Oregon. We called to warn them. The police were notified and posed as mechanics to make the arrest.

Pat sat on the couch, rolling two shotgun shells in his

hands, relaxed and undisturbed by his actions.

Pat served seven years of his 35-year sentence for attempted murder. He got out long enough to meet his daughter for the first time before finding enough trouble to put him away for good.

My Normal Life

Five friends and I piled in an old car, ready for a weekend of party and fun. My 5-year-old daughter was perched on my lap.

"Swing by my grandpa's house," I instructed Don the driver. "I gotta drop my daughter off for Mom to watch."

We all laughed and joked our way to Grandpa's, except for Pam. She sat in the front seat, drunk and depressed. She rambled unintelligible words.

We arrived, and I hopped out with Rachel, running down the stairs to Grandpa's place. Mom and I had just returned to the top of the steps when we heard a gunshot. Chaos broke out in the car, with everyone screaming.

"What happened?" I dashed to the car and peered in. Pam clutched her shoulder with one bloody hand, wailing and waving a gun in the other. Lisa slumped against the rear door, blood trickling from a bullet hole in her throat.

"What happened?" I repeated. "Don, tell me!"

Don's eyes reflected shocked terror. "I'm not sure. Pam was babbling about killing herself. She rifled through the glove box and found the gun. She put it to her head but couldn't keep it steady. As she pulled the trigger, I think it dropped, hitting her first, then Lisa. What do we do?" he cried.

"Amy." I called a friend in a nearby town. "It's too freaky. Pam killed Lisa by accident when she was drunk. She got sent away for involuntary manslaughter." My voice shook. "I can't take it."

"Why not move here for a while? Take some time to pull yourself together," Amy suggested. I lasted a year without touching meth. Instead, I anesthetized myself with rivers of booze.

I returned to my hometown to enroll in a program for my GED. There, I met Jack. Immediately, attraction led to quick sex, which led to inevitable pregnancy. We tried hard to make it work, but even the shared tie of our infant daughter couldn't keep the relationship from unraveling. Jack soon drifted away.

I avoided meth through the entire pregnancy and for eight months after Marissa's birth. But with two daughters to support, I needed a job. I got hired to bartend at a local joint. Within weeks, meth ruled me again.

Crime and Chaos

"Mom, can you watch the kids tonight? Gotta work late." Later, I opened the door to let my mother in. Behind me, the TV blared, kids shouted in play and drug deals buzzed in every room of the cramped apartment. Unwashed dishes and clothing sat in smelly piles throughout the house.

"Thanks, Mom. You're the best," I chirped as I flitted out the door.

I managed to avoid drugs through my pregnancies. Other than that, the need for meth conquered any desire to stay clean. The years passed as I shot 19 of them up my veins.

I tended my children during the day, shooting meth at night. I seldom slept.

I tended bar or babysat other dealers' children to generate income for my next fix.

Eventually, I needed crime to help support my habit. Life whipped into a frenzied parade of theft, arrests, jail time, paper crime, arrests, judges and more jail time. The legal system and I continually fought over custody of my children.

Joy in Jail

My mind cannot compute the number of times I landed in jail. During one of these stays, my cellmate, Lacy, coaxed me, "Come on, Sarah, let's go to the church service."

"I don't want to," I said.

"Hey, I know it isn't our first choice of fun things to do, but it'll kill an hour or more in this boring joint. Let's go," Lacy insisted.

Week after week, Lacy dragged me to the jail church services, ignoring my weak protests. I knew two ladies among the visiting Christians, and it embarrassed me that they saw me in such a condition.

One night after Lacy had done her part in getting me to church, I returned and flopped on my bunk. Weariness permeated my body and soul. Life had disintegrated into a haze of using, dealing, failed attempts to come clean, relapses and promises — a never-ending orbit of chaos.

God, I prayed, *is it true you can change my life, as Darla and Judy keep telling me at those services? Is it true you really love me, even in this stink hole?*

Into my bruised, battered, abused heart sang one divine word. *Yes.*

I didn't weep, shout or laugh. I simply let out a long sigh, releasing years of emptiness and failure into God's hands.

Okay, God, I responded without eloquence. *Okay.*

Joy overtook the weariness, melting it into the sea of God's forgiveness.

The Last Time

"Darla, this is Sarah. Can you take me to church? I can't wait to start my new life as a Christian!"

"My pleasure!" Darla's warm laugh matched the joy in my heart.

"If anyone would like prayer for any situation, please feel free to come up to the altar," Darla's pastor invited. I went forward, crying and crying. I sensed people gathering around me, enfolding me in a blanket of love. Many laid hands on me as prayer rose to God.

One by one, I felt hands and then persons moving away from me until only one person remained. Time passed as she prayed. When I opened my eyes, she enveloped me in a warm embrace. "I have been praying for you a long time," she whispered in my ear.

Michelle became one of my staunchest friends and a mentor. She drove me to church. She tutored me in the Bible. During one of these studies, her face crumpled as she reached for me.

"Sarah." She sobbed. "For years, I blamed you for Nicole's drug use. I thought you were the one who got her hooked. I hated you with all my heart, but God told me I had to pray for you. So I did," she finished with fresh weeping.

"I didn't start her on drugs, but I certainly *was* a bad influence on her once she got hooked, Michelle. I'm so sorry for that. Can you forgive me?" I asked.

We wept long and hard, clinging to each other as years of misunderstanding and hatred drained away.

I had so much going for me. I had become a grandma while in jail. I had three kids and a grandbaby to support.

Soon, it got to be too much, trying to keep it all together on my own. I needed meth, and since I never needed to look for trouble, trouble soon found me. I started using again.

This time as the police hauled me away, I heard Jesus say in my heart, *You're not doing this anymore.*

Deep in my spirit, I knew this day would come and come quickly because God had meant business when I told him *okay* my last time in jail.

I sat on my cot as dejected as a lost dog in the pound, lacing and unlacing my trembling fingers. *Jesus*, I prayed. *This time, I've blown it completely. I'll never be a part of my kids' lives again. Rachel was sent to a drug treatment center. I'm glad for that; she'll get the help she needs.*

Marissa went to her dad's. I'm a little nervous about that. She hasn't seen him since she was a baby. It's been 11 years! Dear God, help that to work out. Jason and Zach are in foster care. I'm so sorry, God. I'm so very sorry.

"Mail," the guard yelled. "Here's one for you, Sarah." She thrust a lone envelope through the bars.

I looked at the return address. From Michelle. I groaned. Michelle kept pushing this program called Teen Challenge on me. *Teen Challenge,* I snorted to myself. *What can they do for me? I'm 35. I don't need some organization. I almost made it last time. I know I can do it the next time.*

Bracing myself, I unfolded the delicate writing paper. "Dear Sarah," Michelle wrote. "Please consider Teen Challenge. You know how much they helped Nicole. I know they can help you, too. You can't make it on your own, no matter how much you think you can. You need the help this organization provides. Think about it!"

Okay, I thought. "Okay," I said out loud.

"Michelle, I promise you when I get out, I'll sign up for Teen Challenge."

If nothing else, to get you off my back, I added to myself.

STRENGTH FOR TODAY

Teen Challenge

"Hello, Sarah, welcome to Teen Challenge." My counselor smiled. She drove me to a lovely house. "The program calls for a year commitment. You will live in a highly structured environment as we work through the reasons for your drug dependency.

"Everyone rises early for devotions and prayer. You will go to the job center to gain life skills. You will not make eye contact with any male in the program. You will raise your hand to use the restroom.

"Later in the program, you will go out with others to speak at churches about Teen Challenge and how it is helping you put your life back together. Any questions?"

True to her word, I found myself standing in front of the congregation of a nearby church. "Hello, my name is Sarah. I'm a former meth addict. I came here tonight to tell you how Teen Challenge is helping me overcome the addiction and get my life back together."

Restoration

"I love you, David, but you have to leave. I'm tired of doing jail time every time the cops catch us together."

David and I had met back when he sold drugs for my mother. I dated him after my son's birth. Soon we shared living quarters, drugs and crime. The court issued a no-contact order, which we ignored, resulting in several jail stays.

Not long after I returned home from Teen Challenge, the phone rang.

"Sarah?" a familiar voice asked.

"David? How are you? Where are you? What are you doing?" Glad questions tumbled from my lips.

"Sarah, do you think I can see you?" he asked.

I called my mentor. "Susan, would it be okay for me to meet with David over Christmas?" I asked.

"I'll okay the visit if you have a chaperone," she replied.

"Could we meet at my mom's house?" I asked.

"That would be good."

"Thank you!"

***

David and I sat smiling at each other on my mother's couch.

"It's so good to see you, David."

"It's good to see you, too, Sarah. I love you. I want to marry you. Will you marry me?" he finished in a rush.

"I'd be so happy to, David, but I have to know — are you still using meth?"

"Yes," he replied, without evasion.

"I'll marry you if you do what you have to do."

"I know. There's a warrant out on me. I'll have to turn myself in. You know, if I do, I'll probably do more time."

"Yeah, you're probably right, but it has to be for us to marry."

David served his time and returned to marry me. We began working hard to put our lives back together in the wake of meth's destructive path.

Eight months after our wedding, I accompanied David on a routine probation visit.

"Please, sit down." The officer waved to two chairs as we entered his office. Minutes later, two detectives walked in.

"We have reason to believe you were involved in the murder of Grant Smith," one stated. "We're here to question you."

More detectives arrived, escorting David's brother, Jack, into the room. The hours crept by as the detectives asked countless questions.

David told the whole truth. "Yes, we did it," he said quietly. My heart stopped. In shock, I listened as my new, wonderful husband revealed secrets hidden for 20 years.

"Jack and I went camping with our two buddies, Rick and George. We were drugging and ran out of drugs. Rick and George ran into town to find more. They had family there.

"They came back with this wild story of some cop snitcher guy messing with kids and stealing from his family. His sister promised us a lot of money and a new car if we'd take him out. We needed the money, man, you know, for the drugs."

David stopped, searching the distant past before resuming his tale. "I did it," he said. "I knocked on his trailer door. When he opened it, I asked, 'Hey, man, are you

Grant Smith?' He said yes."

David halted again. He looked at me, tears forming, and then back to the assembled lawmen. "I yanked out my knife. He fought me but not hard enough. I buried the knife here." David touched the base of his head with one finger. "I knew he was dead," he finished in a whisper.

"I went back to the car. We were all in shock over what we had agreed to do and had just done. We burned the car and our clothing. We never collected the blood money." David released a long sigh. "I'm glad it's over."

Tragedy

With God's help, I got a good job managing an assisted living facility. Marissa came home for good. Rachel got married. Her 4-year-old son and new husband moved in with me. Only two years apart in age, my son, Jason, and Zach became inseparable. Even with David gone, life started looking good.

Rachel and John both got jobs working where I managed. I was proud to see them begin building a solid life for themselves. They decided to move closer to the facility where we all worked. I took the day shift, Rachel the swing shift and John worked at night.

I picked up Zach on my way home from work, taking care of him through Rachel and John's shifts, returning him to his parents on my way back to my own shift.

"Hello, John. It's Sarah." I had called their home. "Can Zach come over for Jason's birthday party?"

"No." John's voice was gruff. "He's over there too much."

I bit back angry words as a sick feeling hit my stomach. *Maybe you're too involved, Sarah,* I lectured myself. *It's time to let the kids be adults.*

"Okay," I said, trying to control the tremble in my voice.

A few hours later, my mom showed up at my door. "Sarah." She sounded scared. "You need to get to Monroe right now. Zach was hurt in a four-wheeler accident."

"What?" I cried, grabbing my keys and dashing to the car. During the 45-minute drive, I called Rachel's cell.

"Rachel," I cried. "This is Mom. Where are you? What happened to Zach?"

"I'm in the ambulance with him right now. He's in a coma from the accident. Meet us at the hospital."

"I'm coming!"

I spotted John as soon as I entered the hospital. I ran over to him. He reeked of alcohol.

Just then, police arrived to question him.

"I accidentally did something," was all they could get out of John. "But I don't remember anything." His behavior caused enough suspicion to take him elsewhere for questioning.

I ran over to the ICU nurse. "I'm Zach's grandmother. Please, may I see my grandson?"

My hand flew to cover my gaping mouth. My darling 4-year-old grandson lay like a broken rag doll, bruised, battered and brain dead.

GOD'S PRINCESS

As the drone of life-support machines hummed in our ears, we signed organ donation papers, passing his life on to others.

Rachel's husband of four months, Zach's stepfather, was convicted on multiple charges, including aggravated murder and torture.

Running Strong

I continue working at the assisted living facility. As I look into the aging faces of elderly people I have come to love, I see years of joy and pain etched there.

God, I have already lived three lifetimes of pain, I think to myself. *It's a miracle I'm even alive. You've helped me overcome the life of meth addiction and all the chaos it created.*

You helped me when David was taken from me. I'm alone again but not really alone because you have promised you will never, never leave me.

My cell rings. I smile. It's Marissa. "Hi, sweetie, how was your day?" I ask.

"Good, Mom. Can I go to the mall with Sherry? Her mom is taking us."

"Sure. Just be home for dinner."

Thank you, God. I smile as I slip the cell into my pocket. *Thank you for reminding me what I have. I thought I would never have my children in my life again, but you brought Marissa back. Rachel is trying to put her life back together. And even though Mom has custody of*

Jason, I have full visitation. He is with me most of the time. How can I thank you for the return of my children?

Every night, I crawl into my big empty bed, hugging pillows instead of my strong, warm husband. Many nights, I cry out of loneliness. I must remind myself that God is always with me.

Jesus, I weep into the pillow, *it is hard being here alone, with David 300 miles away. I can't afford to visit him very often. And it's so hard to have the glass between us. I can't even touch him, receiving warm strength from his hug. Being in his presence without the ability to touch is such sweet agony.*

I know you are with me on my side of the glass, and I know you are with David on his. And he constantly reminds me of how he is using this time to tell the other inmates about you and what you have done for us.

"David, I love you," I breathe into the stillness. "Someday, you will return. Even though it is still years down the road, I know you'll return."

Then the worst emptiness of all hits me: the senseless, cruel murder of my precious grandson at the hands of his stepfather. The tears turn to a torrent. I shove my face deeper into the pillow to stifle my sobs.

Oh, God, oh, Father, I wail, *it's all my fault. Zach is the victim of the drugged life I led for years and passed on to his mother. It's all my fault.*

Sarah, you forget who I am, the Lord gently admonishes me. *I am the Alpha and the Omega. I am the beginning and the end. Nothing good or bad happens in the world without my knowing about it first.*

You're right, Lord. I know you have only good plans for me. You promised me that in Jeremiah 29:11.

I whisper the verse out loud: "'I know the plans I have for you,' declares the Lord, 'plans to prosper you and not to harm you, plans to give you hope and a future.'"

Yes, Lord, I must trust you, even when I don't understand why bad things happen. Only you have the power to make good things happen from bad stuff. Because of Zach's death, other people live. Little Hannah wrote to thank me for Zach's heart and her second chance at life. She is a part of us because Zach is a part of her.

I reach for my Bible and smile through my tears. How life has changed! A few years ago, I'd be reaching for a needle right now to drown myself in meth's false joy. Not anymore.

My hands tremble as I open the book. No matter where I open my Bible, a geyser of God's love, mercy and truth gushes out to cover me with his promises.

I begin reading, inserting my own name to make God's promises more personal to me.

"If the Lord delights in [Sarah's] way, he makes [her] steps firm; though [Sarah] stumble, [she] will not fall, for the Lord upholds [her] with his hand." (Psalm 37:23, 24)

I sigh deeply. *Ah, yes, Lord. You are so much better than the rush of meth. Your "rush" is eternal. I love you so much! Amen.*

FINAL THOUGHTS
By Melanie Widmer

We hope these stories have found a place in your heart. Maybe you saw similarities to your own story. No life is completely untouched by sorrow or loss, but how will your story end?

Jesus, the author of the universe, wants to live your story with you. Imagine — the creator of the earth and stars cares about you more than any person ever has or ever will. How can we go wrong walking hand in hand with the one who truly sees the big picture? It's never too late to start a new chapter.

God is hoping you will accept the gifts he is offering — the gift of eternal life in heaven; of a relationship more beautiful and fulfilling than any other; of forgiveness and restoration. The first step is a conversation, and you can be sure he is listening. This simple prayer, or one like it, can change your life:

Dear Jesus,

I know I need you in my life. I choose today to accept the gift you have for me. Please forgive me for my sins, for the wrong choices I have made. Lord, please help me to hear your voice and follow you in everything I do. Thank you for giving up your own life on a cross for me. From this day, Jesus, I will trust you and live for you. I know you have a plan and a purpose for my life. Help me, Lord, to walk with you.

Amen

We at Living Hope Christian Center would love to walk beside you. We don't have everything all figured out, but we keep leaning on the one who does — the God of happy endings.

I have made you, and I will carry you;
I will sustain you, and I will rescue you.
(Isaiah 46:4)

We would love for you to join us!

We meet Sunday mornings at 10:30 a.m. at
25 NE A Street, P.O. Box 707, Madras, OR 97741.

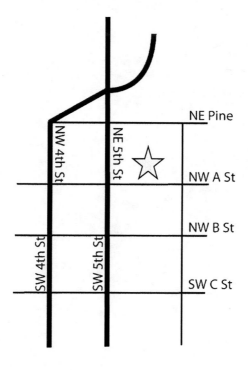

Please call us at 541.475.2405 for directions, or
contact us at www.livinghopecc.com.
Please email us at info@livinghopecc.com.